God So Loved the Third World

THOMAS D. HANKS

God So Loved the Third World

The Biblical Vocabulary of Oppression

TRANSLATED FROM THE SPANISH
BY JAMES C. DEKKER

Wipf and Stock Publishers
EUGENE, OREGON

Wipf and Stock Publishers
199 West 8th Avenue, Suite 3
Eugene, Oregon 97401

For God So Loved the Third World
By Hanks, Tom
ISBN: 1-57910-467-3
Publication date: October, 2000
Previously published by Orbis Books, 1984.

Contents

PART THREE
PROPHETIC PERSPECTIVES AND THE GOSPEL OF THE POOR

Foreword

This work fills a large vacuum in biblical research and exposition. On the one hand it makes a serious, critical, and constructive contribution to the search for an adequate biblical theology on the problem of poverty. On the other hand, coming as it does from an evangelical perspective, it strengthens and at the same time corrects many of the opinions articulated within the various political liberation theologies that have sprung up in Latin America during the last fifteen years.

When Thomas Hanks shows from the Bible that the primary cause of poverty is oppression, and that the corresponding alternative is liberation, he verifies biblically various theses affirmed by liberation theologians. However, when he focuses on poverty as a central biblical theme in both Testaments; when he details how precisely the Bible points to oppression as the root cause of poverty; and when he also suggests full and integral liberation as an ethical and missionary response—when he does these three things, Hanks not only reappropriates the historical relevance of the biblical message, but also calls into question the preeminence that some liberation theologians have given to Marxist concepts at the expense of biblical truth. Speaking from Latin America Hanks thus gives a solid and innovative testimony to the classic Reformed motto *sola scriptura.* This is just another way of saying that in Evangelical theology the Bible occupies first place, and it does so not only because it is the word of *God,* but also because it is the liberating word that God speaks *precisely from* the situation of oppression in which the poor live.

Therefore this book is not merely another treatise in liberation theology that repeats points common to the different streams of Latin American theology. Rather it represents a foundational work of the emerging *radical Evangelical* theology. That is what we call the stream of theology that works within the following parameters of the historical Protestant-Evangelical movement: the normative character of the Bible in the life and mission of the church; a personal experience with the gospel through faith in Jesus Christ; and obeying and communicating the gospel as the way to evince the fruit of life in the Holy Spirit. In this way such a theology attempts to trace those parameters back to their origins and carry them to their final results—all of which make this a prophetic and contextual movement in Latin American Protestantism.

It is prophetic insofar as it denounces the following kinds of theologies: those that claim to be biblical but end up by twisting the Bible's message; those that call for a personal experience of the gospel but resist its call to change personal values; those that insist that the gospel must be spread, but soft-pedal or even deny its incarnational character and its demand for justice. Additionally, this theology is prophetic because it announces a Christian praxis that is more faithful to the biblical message, more holistically oriented as is the gospel itself, more consistent in its ethical demands, and more concerned with and committed to the destiny of those to whom the good news of salvation issues its challenge.

Moreover, this theology is contextual insofar as it attempts to understand the word in terms of the concrete situation of the people of God both in years past and in the present. The faithful interpreter of the Bible is not only to understand the Bible in its *original* context, but also in the context of the life and mission of God's people throughout its history and especially in the *present*. In order to do this the exegete must be in continual dialogue with various students of reality—historians, economists, sociologists, anthropologists, psychologists, and political scientists. But more than anything else, the exegete must be sensitive to the cries of those who suffer poverty and live in it.

In the present book Hanks shows himself to be a biblical theologian who wishes to be faithful to the text in every way. He is open to the contributions of colleagues in other fields, sensitive to the cries of the poor, and concerned to help the people of God in Latin America carry out its mission. Therefore the book is not merely biblical theology, but pastoral theology. It provides much material for sermons and for the development of God's people in evangelization and in diaconal work.

Thus it gives me great pleasure to congratulate the author and recommend his book to all those who are doing pastoral work both in Latin America and elsewhere, and to professors and students of theology.

Orlando E. Costas
Eastern Baptist Seminary
Philadelphia

Preface

Whenever we could not answer a question about the Bible at Wheaton Graduate School of Theology many years ago, the late Dr. Frank Neuberg loved to prod us by asking: "What's the matter? Don't you read your Bible any more? Afraid you'll mess up your theology or something?" Little did I then realize how perceptive was his insight into the problems of our doubly conservative mindset (theological and political) for a disciplined listening to and grasping of the teaching of such subversive literature.

My own serious study—and problems—with the teaching of the Bible about the poor began back in 1969 in an Overseas Training Camp in Costa Rica sponsored by Inter-Varsity. Charles Troutman, who had dedicated his life to student ministry, first in the U.S.A., then in Australia, and finally in Latin America, invited me to prepare a lecture on the biblical teaching on poverty. A simple task, I thought: after working with students myself for six years in Latin America, I realized that preoccupation with the poor was something our students and the Bible had in common. Eager and early, I began my research, confident that in the various biblical dictionaries and encyclopedias I would find long articles and most of the relevant texts needed for the lecture.

Imagine my shock when I consulted work after work of First World biblical erudition—which pretend to treat all the principal themes and virtually all the minor ones in the Bible—and found almost nothing! My initial reaction was one of perplexity, frustration, and indignation. Perplexity, because I could not understand why there should be such a huge lacuna on this matter in my biblical reference works. Frustration, because I would have to do a hundred times the expected work for the lecture—starting almost from zero. And indignation, because I knew about so many enormous doctoral theses in the biblical field on utterly trivial and unimportant themes, whereas the poor, who clamor so loudly for attention in Third World churches, had been virtually ignored—like Lazarus clamoring for attention at the rich man's gate.

Thus with a lecture deadline upon me I began reading through my Bible trying to find all the texts that said something about the poor. Within a week I had arrived at Revelation, deluged with pertinent material. Then came the second great trauma: the struggle to bring some semblance of order to the multitude of texts. In desperation I settled for a simple scheme of "causes" and "solutions." Structured thus the biblical material revealed some shocking gaps that I did my best to remedy with makeshift "interpretations." Even so the results remained highly embarrassing. Ransacking the Bible and repeated plunges into various concordances, such as Young's and Strong's, uncovered not a single text attributing poverty to "underdevelopment" (comfortable code word of the 1960s for racial inferiority). The obvious inherent laziness and multitudinous vices of the poor received only a few passing references, mainly in Proverbs. And our infernal population explosions seemed to be presented obstinately as proof of divine blessing! Worst of all, my already painfully battered Republican nose kept banging into texts that linked poverty to oppression. But, like the pesky intruder in James's churches, "oppression" was, in effect, told to "sit at my feet" or at least "keep its place" in an interminable list of more acceptable causes.

Already it began to dawn on me that my Bible was starting to look like a strangely different book—that in fact I could find very little that did not seem to have *some* relationship to the poor (after all, the gospel itself was directed particularly to them, as Jesus said). With a group of "gringo" students eager for missionary service in Latin America waiting expectantly, I staggered to the lectern at the camp, my briefcase bulging with enough notes to talk for a week!

As I review that outline of my first lecture, I am aware of an ideological perspective imposed by my background: gringo, capitalist—almost Goldwater Republican—that did not make for empathetic reading of subversive literature. However, the lightning strikes from biblical data began to electrocute many cherished presuppositions. Laboring under the tyranny of the urgent (lecture deadline), I had depended almost entirely on common translations, and thus many of the most important texts utterly escaped my attention (*traduttore, traditore,* "translator, traitor," runs the Italian refrain, and never truer than in this case).

The fundamental importance of the exodus as the biblical paradigm of liberation for the oppressed poor did not even occur to me, and for many years I continued expanding and elaborating my outline, never realizing the tremendous distortion caused by this gap in my biblical understanding. Finally, one day in my seminary course on biblical theology, when we had surveyed the multitude of pentateuchal laws relating to the poor, my students—by then avid readers of the liberation theologies—pointed out to me that God had not given all those laws to the pharaoh to make slavery more pleasant—or even to Moses while in Egypt—but only after the "original revolution" of the exodus!

Thereafter, for ten years I kept studying and teaching about the poor in biblical theology—with university groups, professionals, local churches (in both Costa Rica and the U.S.A.), in seminary courses, and finally in some continental seminars. I know I have hardly begun to understand the profundity and wealth of biblical teaching about the poor. However, interest in my conclusions has reached the point of justifying a well-earned "sabbatical" vacation for the mimeograph machine (that has regularly churned out new and ever larger editions of that original outline)—that my conclusions might be published in more permanent form. The chapters of this book represent only a small part of my whole outline on the subject, but they do represent what I consider the most important and original part.

We may be grateful to God that theologians have begun to take seriously what the Scriptures teach about the poor. Even biblical scholars from Europe and North America now often put the poor at the top of their agenda. This new perspective is radically changing the whole orientation of the church, particularly in the Third World. Although it was not their original purpose, the chapters that follow may provide something of a correction of common caricatures about Latin American liberation theologies—distortions that keep cropping up in the most unexpected places. Thus in a three-volume *Dictionary of New Testament Theology* of impeccable erudition we find a respectable article on the "poor," but liberation theologies are relegated to the article on "war"! (Grand Rapids: Zondervan, 1978, vol. 3, pp. 958-82). So be it. But it is worth pointing out that pacifism is much more dominant in Latin American theology in praxis than in the U.S.A., where clergy can bless napalm for Vietnam, call for neutron bombs in Europe, and sing "Onward Christian Soldiers" whenever the marines invade—without provoking even a raised eyebrow in most circles. As the psalmist complained:

Here I am, "peace personified" [*'ani—shalom*] but every time I open my mouth they declare war on me! [120:7].

Professors who have corrected too many student theses and other readers who share my crablike proclivities will be relieved to know that it is not necessary to read the following chapters in their present order: each was written for an independent purpose—as a stubborn remnant of overlap and repetition still bears witness. Hence, if you share my reactionary political and theological background, you may feel more comfortable beginning with the last chapter and proceeding backward.

Chapter 7 is an example of what happens when a seminary professor tries to write an evangelistic tract. A Latin American campus crusade director, starting work in Costa Rica with a survey course at the university, had shared his great problem: of every ten students who rejected his gospel presentation, he reported, nine did so because they saw Christianity and the churches as socially reactionary and supporting an unjust status quo. For Latin America, better start with Luke 4:18–19 instead of John 3:16, I concluded—and expected to finish the tract in two or three days. However, once involved in the fascinating and troublesome exegesis of Luke 4:18–19, the task dragged on for several months. In the process I had also written chapter 6 to account for some of the exegetical problems encountered in Luke 4. This chapter represents a new interpretation of Isaiah 58 and supplies part of the evidence for the interpretation of Luke 4. It was submitted to a prestigious biblical journal during the debate on the Panama Canal treaties, but was fired back in record time because of the dreadful contamination of its exegesis by Third World ideological prejudices.

Even with chapter 6 sanitarily excised I cannot pretend to be content with chapter 7 as an "evangelistic effort"—nor are my colleagues in Minamundo (Ministry to the Student and Professional World), many of them genuinely gifted evangelists. However, I still believe it gives an idea of the way the new perspectives on the poor in biblical theology must transform our evangelism (and I refer as much to the *content* of the message as to the methods commonly utilized, not to mention the inescapable ecclesiastical reality that too often hampers receptivity). Many evangelicals here have commented on the implications of the fact that, when one of our *best* evangelists held a campaign a few years ago in Nicaragua, President Somoza gladly helped defray campaign expenses. Such a fact—hardly an isolated instance in Latin America—raises the suspicion that something has gone wrong with our comprehension of the gospel. When John the Baptist preached the good news of the kingdom, the Roman government (quite superior to that of Somoza) imprisoned and beheaded him. When Jesus preached his good news to the poor, he was crucified. Peter and Paul were always getting carted off to prison. But when we preach our revised, apolitical version, dictators and tyrants are eager to help us cover the costs! This anomaly has even fundamentalist and dispensational theologians in Latin America starting to ask whether our "made in U.S.A." version of the gospel has not changed and emasculated the message some way. Everything we say may appear exceedingly good and biblical. But instead of "making low the mountains and elevating the valleys" have we managed to bury the "stone of stumbling"?

Chapter 5, on Isaiah 53, represents a revision of a paper originally prepared for a seminary course on messianic prophecy. It seeks to show how the new theological perspectives in Latin America help us interpret the gospel more faithfully in a continent racked by poverty and oppression. Like chapter 6, it establishes a certain exegetical and theological basis for the way the gospel is presented in chapter 7. Moreover it shows that acceptance of previously unrecognized elements in biblical theology in no way need cause us to deny the fundamental elements of our theological heritage. Rather, I should insist, evangelical elements regain their true dignity and force when interpreted in the light of their original context in the life of God's oppressed people in biblical times.

Finally, for crabs of a particularly persistent species, chapters 1–3 were originally prepared for the Consultation on Biblical Theology of the Latin American Theological Fraternity (Buenos Aires, 1978). They represent an amplification of one factor (oppression) that I believe biblical theology represents as the basic cause of poverty. When I first prepared those lectures, the utter absence of serious treatment of a theme so dominant in biblical theology astounded me. The reader impatient with the technical apparatus of scientific exegesis (Hebrew, Greek, lexicons, and the like—another deplorable extension of the technological society, I am afraid Jacques Ellul would say) might well read the introductions and conclusions of these chapters and leap to the following chapters. However, those who take the time to look up all the texts on oppression in the Bible, and mark the possible alternative translations, will have a radically new perspective on the biblical message and the Third World-type context in which it was written. They may also begin to understand why ideologically uncontaminated First World biblical erudition feels so threatened by emerging Latin American theologies that they deal with us in articles on warfare.

Knowing how very hard it has been for me to teach the Bible in a context buffeted by gusty winds (charismatic revival, liberation theologies, Sandinista revolution), I can only pray that readers more sheltered may read these pages with mind, heart, and Bible open. I realize that much may appear new and shocking to any who share my conservative background. But if we, like the disciples in Berea, "search the Scriptures to see if these things are certain" (Acts 17:11), I believe we shall have to rebuke our traditional tomes of biblical and theological erudition in the words of the Queen of Sheba to Solomon: "Not even half was told me" (1 Kings 10:7).

Particularly those of us who call ourselves evangelicals and seek above all to be "biblical Christians" ought not to reject the new perspectives in biblical understanding that are streaming forth from the Third World. Have we not always insisted and believed that "God yet has much new light to break forth from his word"? If this is what is happening in our own days, we should be the first to rejoice in this new light and seek to walk in it (see John 1:5–7). I know that for me personally, after eighteen years teaching in a Latin American context, the Bible is a new book. Opportunities for service in a reformatory, literacy teaching in a nearby slum, and dialogical biblical exposition with Christian social workers in Latin America leave me convinced that the Bible is incredibly more true than most defenders of inerrancy ever realize.

In my seminary preparation in the U.S.A., I never dreamed I was preparing for a career as a professor of "subversive literature"! Now I am not surprised when I hear how the American Bible Society landed in trouble for publishing a modern, comprehensible translation of Amos with a red cover and the simple word "Justice" printed on the cover (banned in Pinochet's Chile). Or that the use of a Spanish version of Mary's Magnificat in the Catholic Mass was prohibited in one area of Argentina (some things are best left in Latin!). But the Lord who "makes all things new" is beginning, with our understanding of his word, to make of his people a "people prepared."

Seminario Bíblico Latinoamericano
San José, Costa Rica

Acknowledgments

To Orlando Costas, without whose vision, encouragement, and continued counsel these chapters would have remained scattered occasional pieces, little known in Spanish, and utterly unknown in English.

To Jim Dekker, fellow missionary, who enthusiastically undertook the formidable job of translation and provided numerous additional insights, especially (in chap. 3) regarding the interpretation of the Acts of the Apostles.

To Linda Holland, co-worker in Costa Rica, whose magic typewriter for many years has turned my ugly drafts—both Spanish and English—into beautiful manuscripts, and who crowned her labors by discovering in her own study of the Bible a term for oppression that I had missed.

To esteemed colleagues and students in the Seminario Bíblico Latinoamericano who, since 1963, patiently sought to help an obtuse, often bewildered, "gringo" understand what Latin America and its liberation theologies are all about.

To Bill Jerman, whose wizardry as editor produced countless corrections and improvements to make the book more comprehensible for English readers.

To John Eagleson and the team at Orbis Books, for their courage and ecumenical spirit in accepting an odd book rather raucously Protestant at many spots and granting it full freedom to make its protests known—even when it "doth protest too much."

To my wife, Joyce, whose years of university teaching, research, and writing in French literature, biblical studies, and theology—most recently with Jacques Ellul—have provided an unfailing stream of insights and corrections to my understanding of the word of God and the modern world.

And to our son, Stanley, and our daughter, Elizabeth, who have been "uprooted and replanted," ever willing to tackle a new language and make new friends. Without their patient endurance and helpful spirit, all parental bookwriting would have been impossible.

Acronyms and Abbreviations

AB, Anchor Bible

BDB, Francis Brown, S.R. Driver, and Charles A. Briggs, *A Hebrew and English Lexicon of the Old Testament* (Oxford: Clarendon, 1907)

cj, conjectural

Hol., William L. Holladay, ed., *A Concise Hebrew and Aramaic Lexicon of the Old Testament* (Grand Rapids: Eerdmans, 1971)

JB, Jerusalem Bible

KB², Ludwig Koehler and Walter Baumgartner, *Lexicon in Veteris Testamenti Libros* (Leiden: Brill, 2nd ed., 1958)

MT, Massoretic text

LXX, Septuagint

NAB, New American Bible

NEB, New English Bible

NIV, New International Version

RSV, Revised Standard Version

PART ONE

OPPRESSION IN
THE OLD TESTAMENT

Chapter 1

Basic Old Testament Vocabulary
of Oppression

OPPRESSION: A BASIC STRUCTURAL CATEGORY
OF BIBLICAL THEOLOGY

Perhaps more than anyone else, Hugo Assmann has stressed the importance
of oppression or domination as the primary cause of Third World poverty and
also as the starting point for Latin American liberation theologies. This theme
runs as a leitmotif through his book *Theology for a Nomad Church:*

> The historical incidence of the language of "liberation" in the Latin
> American Church is linked to the growing awareness of our situation as
> *oppressed* peoples [p. 37; italics added].
>
> Perhaps the greatest merit of the theology of liberation is its insistence
> on the starting point of its reflection: the situation of *"dominated"*
> [Latin] America" [p. 38; italics added].
>
> We are beginning to realize what we are in history: not merely
> underdeveloped peoples in the sense of "not yet sufficiently developed,"
> but peoples "kept in a state of underdevelopment": dominated and
> *oppressed* peoples—which is a very different thing [p. 49; italics added].
>
> More than anything else the personal experience of belonging to
> dominated nations has produced the theology of liberation [p. 52].
>
> One thing virtually all the documents so far published agree on is that
> the starting point of the theology of liberation is the present historical
> situation of dominance and dependence in which the countries of the
> Third World find themselves [p. 53].

Furthermore Assmann insists that awareness of oppression must be the
foundation of any contemporary theology:

3

If the state of domination and dependence, in which two-thirds of
humanity live with an annual toll of thirty million dead from starvation
and malnutrition, does not become the starting point for *any* Christian
theology today, even in the affluent and powerful countries, then
theology cannot begin to relate meaningfully to the real situation. Its
questions will lack reality and not relate to real men and women [p. 54].[1]

Two questions arise in the face of such statements and such a theology: (1) Is
this Latin American theology, which uses as its starting point the situation of
oppression and domination, something entirely new? (2) Is there a biblical
basis that warrants emphasizing so strongly the situation of oppression?

Anyone who has read much in the theological classics (Augustine, Luther,
Calvin, Barth, Berkouwer et al.) will recognize that the theme of oppression
has received little or no attention there. One might think that the Bible says
little about oppression. Furthermore, one searches in vain for the theme in
Bible dictionaries, encyclopedias, and the like.

However, when we strike the rock of a complete Bible concordance, to our
great surprise we hit a gusher of texts and terms that deal with oppression! In
short, we find *a basic structural category of biblical theology.*

If we reflect on the Bible writers' historical contexts, we shall understand
why they speak so often about oppression.

The patriarchs entered the Holy Land as immigrants, a social class commonly oppressed, along with widows and orphans, as we shall see later.

Biblical theology recognizes the exodus—not the creation—as the central
Old Testament doctrine (comparable to the cross in the New Testament). And
it was precisely in the exodus that an oppressed people won its freedom.

During the time of the judges, Israel repeatedly fell under the yoke of
foreign powers, until finally it chose the monarchy. Even under Solomon
Israel began to feel the weight of internal oppression, as Samuel had warned (1
Sam. 8). During the divided kingdom, both North and South repeatedly
suffered oppression by national oligarchies that commonly collaborated with
the dominant foreign empires—Assyria, Egypt, Babylon, and, after the Exile,
Persia, Greece, and Syria.

The whole New Testament was written with Israel under the boot heel of the
Roman Empire. It would be no exaggeration to say that throughout 90 percent
of its history, Israel was a small, weak nation dominated by great empires,
commonly with a local oligarchy collaborating to maintain the oppressive
status quo.

Throughout the entire history of God's people, then, the times were few and
short when domination and oppression, both foreign and domestic, did not
characterize Israel's politico-economic situation. We should not be surprised,
therefore, that oppression and the resulting poverty receive so much attention
in the literature that recounts Israel's life and struggles. If post-Constantinian
theologies and learned biblical studies do not faithfully expound biblical

teaching on oppression and poverty, it is just one more sign that a church captive to oppressive power structures misses much that is basic in the Scriptures' message. We need not be uncritical of certain extremes, but we should be deeply grateful to Latin American theologians for having pointed us in the direction of a theology more faithful to divine revelation.

TEN BASIC HEBREW ROOTS FOR "OPPRESSION"

§1. Oppression Means Injustice—*'ashaq*

The most important and basic Hebrew words that express the experience of oppression come from the verb *'ashaq* (37 times) and include the noun *'osheq* (15 times), in addition to four other words that occur less frequently (7 times).[2] In all we find 59 uses of this word family in the Old Testament.

'ashaq is related to an Arabic word that means "harshness, roughness" or "injustice." The biblical contexts in which *'ashaq* appears frequently show some kind of injustice, force, or violence. Lexicons basically agree in giving "oppress" as the first meaning of *'ashaq* and "to take by extortion" as the second.

A verse from Ecclesiastes in which words from the *'ashaq* family occur three times nicely illustrates this meaning:

> Again I saw all the oppressions *('ashuqim)* that are practiced under the sun. And behold, the tears of the oppressed *('ashaq)*, and they had no one to comfort them! On the side of the oppressors *('ashaq)* there was power, and there was no one to comfort them [4:1, RSV].

Webster's concisely defines oppression as: "the unjust or cruel exercise of power or authority." Ecclesiastes focuses on the common link between unjust distribution of power and the experience of oppression, which is the abuse of power. Moreover, its repeated cry "there was no comfort" *(nhm)* laments the lack of justice just mentioned in 3:16.[3]

But the psalmist, who does not limit his perspective to what is "under the sun," may seem to contradict flatly the pessimistic point of view of Ecclesiastes:

> The Lord [Yahweh, Lord of the exodus] works justice *(tsedeqah)* and just judgments *(mishpatim)* in favor of all [!] who are oppressed *('ashaq)*. He made known his ways to Moses, his acts to the people of Israel [Ps. 103:6, 7].

Here we can clearly see the relationship between oppression and justice. Far from presenting a God who supports an unjust status quo, the psalmist speaks to us of a God who constantly fosters a kind of revolution against all injustices and oppression ("put down the mighty from their thrones and exalted those of low degree," as in the Magnificat, Luke 1:52).

According to the psalmist the exodus shows us once and for all *what kind of God* Yahweh is ("his ways," Ps. 103:6). Yahweh's work in human history is not limited to Israel (or to the church): "His kingdom rules over all" (v. 19). The psalmist also positively states that Yahweh's work in history concerns "all the oppressed"—a perspective that ought to amaze us because it requires that we totally revise our view of human history. The frontiers of the kingdom must not be equated with those of the church; rather they are the cutting edge of justice and authentic liberation in the world. As Rubem Alves writes:

> The exodus was the experience that molded the consciousness of the people of Israel. It became the structuring principle that determined its way of organizing its time and space. It is not just something in the consciousness of Israel: if it were, it would be just another piece of information. It is more than that; it is the structuring principle because it determined the logic with which Israel assimilated the facts of its historical experience, and the principle by which it organized them and interpreted them. The exodus did not remain as a past experience, something that happened at a particular time in a particular place. It became the paradigm for the interpretation of all space and all time.[4]

This is exactly what the psalmist wants us to notice; in the exodus God revealed his *ways* to Moses—that is, his characteristic activity, no matter what time, place, or people may be involved (Amos 9:7). In a nutshell the "foreign policy" of the kingdom of God is not paranoically "anticommunist." It is projustice: justice on the side of the oppressed.

Psalm 103 thus gives us a revolutionary perspective concerning God's role in human history. But because this psalm does not carefully trace the relationship between oppression and poverty, we must consider another psalm that classically expresses the children of Israel's messianic hopes:

> Give the king thy just judgments, O God,
>   and thy justice to the royal son!
> May he judge thy people with justice
>   and thy poor with just judgments.
> Let the mountains bear prosperity for the people,
>   and the hills, in justice!
> May he defend the cause of the poor of the people,
>   give deliverance to the needy,
>   and crush the oppressor *('ashaq)*. . . .
> For he delivers the needy when he calls,
>   the poor and him who has no helper.

He has pity on the weak and the needy,
    and saves the lives of the needy.
From oppression *(tōk)* and violence he redeems their life;
    and precious is their blood in his sight [Ps. 72:1-4, 12-14].

Again, of course, the oppressor stands opposed to God's justice. By using three synonymns for "poor" *('ani, 'ebyon, dal)* a total of eight times, along with two words for "oppression," the psalmist shows us how closely related poverty and oppression are in Hebrew thought—and also how basic the liberation of the poor from oppression is to the mission and just rule of the awaited messiah! God identifies himself with the poor and the weak (v. 2) and calls them *his* people.

We must also notice what this psalm teaches about violence: the ideal king whom the people await will oppose institutionalized violence by crushing the oppressor (v. 4) in order to rescue the poor and the weak (v. 14). Such institutionalized violence, far from being a Marxist invention, is roundly denounced in the prophets:

And I said:
Hear, you heads of Jacob
and rulers of the house of Israel!
Is it not for you to know justice?—
you who hate the good and love the evil,
who tear the skin from off my people,
and their flesh from their bones;
who eat the flesh of my people,
and flay their skins from them,
and break their bones in pieces,
and chop them up like meat in a kettle,
like flesh in a caldron [Mic. 3:1-3].

Of the 59 uses in the Old Testament of the verb *'ashaq* and related words, poverty is indicated in the context in about half the occurrences (31 times; see note 2, above).

Proverbs reveals another dimension in the relationship between poverty and oppression:

He who oppresses *('ashaq)* a poor man *(dal)* insults his Maker,
but he who is kind to the needy *('ebyon)* honors him [14:31].

According to this text God identifies so fully with the poor that to do them a favor is considered an act of worship *(kabed*—"to honor, glorify"), a doctrine that culminates in the New Testament story of the incarnation (Luke 1 and 2) and in Jesus' teaching of the final judgment (Matt. 25:40). God does not remain indifferent in the face of the struggles and tensions between poor and rich. He identifies himself completely, commits himself to the cause of an oppressed people, and requires his followers to do the same. Thus it is clear that in its original biblical context, the doctrine of creation does not support certain "orders of creation" in order to maintain an unjust status quo. On the contrary, according to the Bible the doctrine of creation is "democratic" and "revolutionary." This is especially evident if we compare the hierarchical and tyrannical context and content of other ancient Near Eastern creation accounts.

§2. Oppression Enslaves—*yanah*

Yanah comes from an Arabic verb that means "to be weak," and it occurs some 19 times in the Old Testament (20 times if we include Ps. 123:4, where there is a textual problem).[5] Poverty is indicated in the context in 15 of the 20 occurrences. The lexicons give as meanings "oppress" or "be violent." The idea of violence is clear in various uses of the word ("the sword of the oppressor," Jer. 46:16; 50:16), and especially indicates institutionalized violence (Zeph. 3:1; cf. vv. 3, 4).

Von Rad suggests that the word literally means "to reduce to slavery; to enslave,"[6] a meaning that applies in practically all uses. The verb almost always appears in contexts that mention the poor, immigrants, widows, and orphans as victims of oppression, inasmuch as they are weak and vulnerable to such abuse. The three uses of the verb in connection with the Jubilee give additional support to von Rad's definition (Lev. 25:14, 17; Ezek. 46:18; cf. v. 17).

Probably the most important use of *yanah* occurs in the radical demand of Deuteronomy 23:

> You shall not give up to his master a slave who has escaped from his master to you; he shall dwell with you, in your midst, in the place which he shall choose within one of your towns, where it pleases him best; you shall not oppress him *(yanah)* [in the sense of enslave; 23:16–17(15–16)].

The oppression referred to here is obviously that which would reenslave someone who had escaped—that is, return them to their original owner, or enslave them again in their new situation. Such a provision was unique in the ancient Near East: the common practice was to return escaped slaves to their former owners. (The Code of Hammurabi even imposed the death penalty on someone who sheltered an escaped slave.) We may compare the Dred Scott Decision (1857) in which the U.S. Supreme Court, contrary to Deuteronomy 23:15–16, refused to protect the rights of escaped slaves. Historians view that fatal decision as one of the main causes of the Civil War. The deuteronomic provision also helps us understand Paul's policy in regard to escaped slaves

(Philemon). By returning Onesimus to his master, the apostle fulfilled the unjust legal demands of the Roman empire, but he did not deny the need for more radical and just laws (such as that of Deuteronomy), had it been possible (1 Cor. 7:21).

The prophet Ezekiel, both an exile and immigrant in Babylon, uses *yanah* more than any other biblical writer and clearly shows the relationship between oppression and poverty. In his great chapter on individual responsibility, the prophet repeatedly insists that the just person must be generous with the poor and not enslave them *(yanah;* 18:7, 12, 16). When Judah did not fulfill these divine requirements, the nation was carried into captivity, because:

> the people of the land have practiced oppression *('ashaq)* and committed robbery ["robbery" when the rich insist on perpetuating unjust social structures]; they have enslaved *(yanah)* the poor and needy, and have oppressed *('ashaq)* the immigrant without redress [22:29; cf. vv. 30, 31].

§3. Oppression Animalizes—*nagas*

The third Hebrew root denoting oppression, common in Exodus and Isaiah, is theologically important because it most often describes the oppression that the Israelites suffered in the exodus.[7] Isaiah uses *nagas* both to show why the Messiah needed to be born (Isa. 9:3) and to specify the sufferings of the "oppressed" Servant (Isa. 53:7).

Nagas occurs 23 times in the Old Testament; 20 times with poverty in the context. Etymologically it is related to an Arabic word (meaning "rouse up [game], roughly force"), to a South Arabic word ("impose tribute") and probably to a Ugaritic word ("overwhelm with work"). Biblical uses of *nagas* reflect all these ideas.

When God answers Job from the tempest, *nagas* points to the freedom of the wild ass that laughs at the noises of the cities and "is deaf to the driver's *(nagas)* shouting" (Job 39:7). Such texts suggest that when persons suffer oppression, they lose their human dignity and are degraded to animal-like existence. Instead of enjoying the dignity and freedom God intended for them as his image bearers (Gen. 1:27, 28), others lord it over them.

The frequent use of *nagas* in Exodus to describe the Pharaoh's overseers who oppressed the Israelites (Exod. 3:7; 5:6, 10, 13, 14; cf. Job 3:18; Zech. 9:8) possibly reflects the Ugaritic etymology ("overwhelm with work"). Such texts emphasize that oppression commonly occurs in the area of physical labor, as the New Testament also warns us (James 5:4–6).

Many uses of *nagas* indicate how tampering with the economic structures leads to oppression. According to the deuteronomic laws, every seven years there was to be a year of release for all debtors. When the rich did not free the debtors in the year of release, they thereby became guilty of oppressing (Deut. 15:2, 3; cf. Isa. 58:3). Heavy tribute imposed by the national oligarchy or by great empires was another form of oppression (2 Kings 23:35; Isa. 3:15; 9:3; 14:2, 4; 60:17; Zech. 10:4; Dan. 11:20). Among these texts the reference in Isaiah 9:3[4] is especially important: the prophet proclaims freedom from Assyria's oppressive yoke through the birth of the Messiah:

> For you have shattered the yoke that burdened them,
> the collar that lay heavy on their shoulders,
> the oppressor's *(nagas)* goad, as on the day of Midian's defeat. . . .
> For a child has been born for us, a son given to us,
> to bear the symbol of dominion on his shoulder;
> and he shall be called
> wonderful in purpose, mighty God *('el gibbor),*
> Father for all time, Prince of Peace [9:3(4), 5(6)].

Many Christmas sermons on verse 6 have been taken out of context. How many preachers have completely ignored the revolutionary implications of oppression as it related to "because"/"for" (Hebrew: *ki,* vv. 3, 4, 5 [4, 5, 6])! According to Isaiah the Messiah's *birth* (not just his second coming) signals an end to foreign oppression. The prophecies that Luke incorporated into his gospel (1:32, 33, 52–55, 67–79) did not ignore this political dimension. When the church postpones liberation from oppression until the Second Coming, it openly contradicts not only the Old Testament prophets but also the New Testament's proclamation of the good news in which the end of oppression is related to the Messiah's *birth.* That is, the kingdom of God that arrived with the birth of Jesus signals the end of all tyranny and oppression. ("Let princes hear and be afraid," Calvin, *Institutes,* IV, xx, 31.) All the covenant blessings, signified by the Old Testament covenant promises, find their fulfillment in the integral liberation Christ brings (2 Cor. 1:20).

For the use of *nagas* in relation to the Suffering-Oppressed Servant (Isa. 53:7), see chapters 2 and 5, below.

§4. The Pain that the Oppressed Feel–*lahats*

Lahats is a picturesque word that literally means "press" or "squeeze," although lexicons also define it as "oppress."[8] The best example of the literal use occurs in the story of Balaam. On seeing the angel of the Lord blocking the narrow path, Balaam's ass "pushed against the wall and pressed *(lahats)* Balaam's foot against the wall" (Num. 22:25).

The expected response to a painful "squeeze" is a "cry." As in the case of *nagas, lahats* is used to describe the oppression Israel suffered in Egypt. Yahweh tells Moses:

> And now, behold, the cry of the people of Israel has come to me, and I have seen the oppression *(lahats)* [noun] with which the Egyptians oppress *(lahats)* [verb] them [Exod. 3:9].

In other words, the Israelites were not living in slavery because they were an "underdeveloped" nation, but rather because the Egyptians were oppressing them—they were "putting the squeeze" on them. Being the most powerful empire of that time, Egypt could easily do just that. But God sided with the poor. In response to his people's outcry (prayers, Exod. 3:7), he began the process of liberation.

Many of the 31 uses of *laḥats* (verb and noun) in the Old Testament tell how God freed his people from oppression *in answer to their outcry* (their prayers; besides Exod. 3:9, see Judg. 2:18, 4:3, 10:12; 2 Kings 13:4; Deut. 26:7; Ps. 42:10, 43:2). In other words, the biblical theology of oppression is not purely humanistic or horizontal. Prayer to the personal, infinite God plays a decisive role in whatever biblical strategy arises to topple oppression. Nevertheless we should note that these texts apparently do not distinguish between "prayer" consciously directed to God and "spontaneous *outcries*" of those who suffer: God hears both. Should we perhaps broaden our understanding of prayer in biblical usage according to these verses?

The bitter experience of oppression in Egypt formed a lasting part of Israel's memory and psychology and developed into a norm for its behavior:

> You shall not oppress *(laḥats)* the stranger; you know the heart of a stranger, for you were strangers in the land of Egypt [Exod. 23:9].

Thus, even within the book of Exodus the oppression/liberation experience begins to function as a paradigm. Later, when God let Israel prosper, he required that they maintain strong solidarity with the poor and the oppressed. Undoubtedly this is part of what Jesus had in mind when he described his disciples as "poor in spirit" (Matt. 5:3), those who hunger and thirst for justice (5:6), and are compassionate to the needy (5:7).[9]

§5. Oppression Crushes—*ratsats*

Ratsats literally means "crush, grind, pound," and figuratively "oppress."[10] We see the literal sense very clearly in Judges when a woman manages to throw a millstone from a tower down on Abimelech's head and "crush" his skull (9:53; cf. Ps. 74:13b–14a). The word well expresses the brutal results of oppression. Of its 20 uses in the Old Testament, poverty is indicated in the context 9 times.

In the first of the great Servant Songs, Isaiah uses *ratsats* twice when describing the Servant's mission:

> Behold my servant, whom I uphold,
> my chosen, in whom my soul delights;
> I have put my Spirit upon him,
> he will bring forth justice to the nations.

> He will not cry or lift up his voice,
>   or make it heard in the street;
> a crushed *(ratsats)* reed he will not break,
>   and a dimly burning wick he will not quench;
>   he will faithfully bring forth justice.
> He will not burn dimly or be crushed *(ratsats)*
>   till he has established justice in the earth;
>   and the coastlands wait for his law [42:1-4].

This text, which the New Testament sees fulfilled in Jesus' mission, deserves careful study, but we must limit ourselves here to points especially important for our theme.

First, what do the crushed reed and smoldering wick refer to? As E. J. Young indicates, the reed seems to refer to the weak, no matter what their nationality. Moreover, the fact that it is crushed *(ratsats)* shows how they suffer oppression.[11] The wick, according to the parallelism of the Hebrew poetry, also refers to the oppressed of any nation who are at the point of despair.[12] Young's interpretation of the reed and wick as metaphors for the poor and oppressed of any nation is supported (1) by the use of *ratsats,* oppression, the unjust use of power; (2) by the triple reference to the lack of justice, the failing the servant comes to correct (vv. 1, 3, 4); and (3) by parallel references in Isaiah where the Messiah's work is to bring justice to the poor and oppressed (11:3b-5; cf. 58:6). The paradigmatic function of the exodus is evident in these contexts—it applies to all nations. In view of the charismatic explosion in Latin America, we should notice that the *only* manifestation of the Holy Spirit's baptism that this text points to is *not* speaking in tongues, but doing justice for the poor and oppressed of all nations (vv. 1, 3, 4; cf. 11:2-5; 61:1-2).

In Luke 4:18-19 Jesus used another text employing *ratsats* from Isaiah to define his mission but theologians have not given it the attention it deserves.[13] Few have noticed that in quoting Isaiah 61:1-2, when he reads the Scriptures in Nazareth's synagogue at the beginning of his public ministry, Jesus also inserts the phrase employing *ratsats* from Isaiah 58:6, where we read:

> Is not this the fast that I choose:
> to loose the bonds of wickedness,
> to undo the thongs of the yoke,
> to let the oppressed-crushed *(ratsats)* go free
> and to break every yoke?
> Is it not to share your bread with the hungry,
> and bring the homeless into your house;
> when you see the naked, to cover him,
> and not to hide yourself from your own flesh? [58:6-7].

Both Isaiah 61:1-2 and 58:6 refer to the Year of Jubilee, when slaves were freed and (in a radical program of agrarian reform) all properties were returned to their original owners (Lev. 25). That was how the law of Moses planned to eliminate social injustices and oppression and to avoid extremes of wealth and poverty in Israel. In Luke 4:19 Jesus ends his quote from Isaiah 61:1–2 with the words "the acceptable year of the Lord," thus stressing the Year of Jubilee that characterized his mission. However, in order to be sure that no one misunderstood what he was trying to explain, Jesus stressed his point by inserting the key liberating phrase of Isaiah 58:6 when reading 61:1–2. In treating Isaiah 58:6 we limit ourselves here to the following conclusions that help us understand Jesus' mission.

First, in Luke 4:18–19, when Jesus describes the life of the poor, he calls attention to the role of oppression. He does not here deal with sin primarily in individualistic or pietistic terms (sex, alcohol, drugs) but in socio-economic terms of oppression, the brutal crushing of personalities and human bodies—things that the rich do to the poor, that the strong do to the weak.

Second, a basic part of Jesus' mission is revolutionary social change that frees the poor and oppressed and restores their dignity and their land. The liberation Jesus came to introduce destroys oppressive social structures ("break every yoke") so that it is impossible to return to slavery. We may compare this with Jeremiah 34, which tells us how the oligarchy in Jerusalem freed their slaves when the Babylonians threatened the city, only to reenslave them when the siege was temporarily lifted.

Finally, we ought to note that such acts of *personal* charity mentioned in verse 7 (feeding the hungry, housing the homeless, clothing the naked, befriending the friendless) ought to be the building blocks erected on the foundation of a decisive liberation—never a substitute for social and structural changes.

In another key text employing *ratsats,* Amos emphasizes the relationship between oppression and poverty using this unforgettable image:

> Hear this word, you cows of Bashan,
> who are in the mountain of Samaria,
> who oppress the poor, who crush *(ratsats)* the needy,
> who say to their husbands, "Bring, that we may drink!" [Amos 4:1].

To be oppressed is like being sat on by a fat cow! What is disturbing about this text is that the wealthy, self-centered women whom the prophet compares to the sleek cows of Bashan apparently were totally unaware of the devastating suffering they caused; undoubtedly their alcoholism aided their oblivion. If they were representatives of their class, as would appear to be the case, their lifestyle probably protected them from having much contact with the poor and oppressed. As Ronald J. Sider comments:

> They may never have realized clearly that their gorgeous clothes and spirited parties were possible only because of the sweat and tears of toiling peasants. In fact they may even have been kind on occasion

to individual peasants they met. (Perhaps they gave them "Christmas baskets" once a year.)[14]

Nevertheless Amos strives to point out that God held them responsible for their own ignorance, indifference, and lifestyle. Sider concludes:

> If one is a member of a privileged class that profits from structural evil and if one does nothing to try to change things, one stands guilty before God. Social evil is just as displeasing to God as personal evil. And it affects more people and is more subtle.[15]

§6. Oppression Kills—*daka'*

We should probably regard *daka'* as the strongest Hebrew word denoting oppression.[16] Both literally and etymologically *daka'* means "pulverize, crush." We find examples of this literal sense in Job 4:18, "pulverized like a moth," and Psalm 90:3, "Thou turnest man back to pulverization *(daka')* and sayest, 'Turn back, O children of men!' "

Including its five cognates, *daka'* occurs 31 times in the Old Testament (10 times with the poor), always emphasizing the fatal results of oppression. Oppression smashes the body and crushes the human spirit. That is, God's image is pulverized like a moth crushed under a boot heel.

Frequently the biblical authors clearly relate this pulverizing oppression to poverty. Although translations do not normally make clear the literal connections, *daka'* and its cognates occur often in Psalms 9 and 10 (which are considered to be one psalm in the Vulgate and subsequent translations). Yahweh is called "a stronghold for the oppressed *(dak)*" in 9:9, who are described as "poor"/"oppressed" *('ani)* in 9:13[12], the "needy" *('ebyon)* and "poor" *('aniwim)* in 9:19[18]. Psalm 10 mentions the "poor" *('ani)* in verses 1, 9 (twice), and 12 (cf. vv. 18 and 17) and, as an example of this class, the orphan in vv. 14 and 18. The poor are called "*oppressed*" in vv. 10 and 18 *(daka'* and *dak,* respectively). *Tōk,* another word for oppression, appears in 10:7.

An examination of Psalms 9 and 10 shows clearly that the poor and the oppressed are thought of as one group or class. In other words, the poor became poor and continue to be poor basically because of pulverizing oppression. As H. J. Kraus observes, this neglected psalm, so eloquent in its portrayal of the plight of the oppressed poor, shows that "back in the oldest time of her history Israel attained the certainty that Yahweh in a special way turns to the underprivileged, the legally victimized and disadvantaged in life's battle and takes them under his protection."[17] However, as Isaiah makes clear to the beleaguered postexilic community, authentic holiness stoops to liberate. Yahweh not only *turns to,* or takes sides with, the oppressed poor in life's battles (class struggle?), he *dwells* permanently with them:

For thus says the one who is high and lifted up
  who inhabits eternity, and whose name is Holy [cf. Isa. 6],
"I dwell in the high and holy place,
  but also by the side of the pulverized-oppressed *(daka')*
  and the bowed down of spirit
to keep alive the spirit of the ones bowed down
  and to make live the heart of the pulverized-oppressed *(daka')*"
                                      [57:15; cf. Ps. 113].

This oracle of liberation clearly points toward and prepares us for the shocking socio-economic context of the incarnation (Luke 1–2), as well as Jesus' teaching about the final judgment (Matt. 25:31–46). The pulverizing oppression expressed by *daka'* also occurs twice in Isaiah 53 (vv. 5, 10) to express the fatal oppression of the Suffering Servant (see below, chap. 2 and 5).

§7. Oppression Humiliates—*'anah*

More than any other word, *'anah* expresses something of the devastating psychological impact of oppression.[18] Of the 82 uses in the Old Testament, *'anah* is used most often in the piel (intensive) root. For this root the lexicons suggest such meanings as "oppress," "humiliate," "make someone feel dependent." It can also mean "be humbled (in fasting)" and "rape." It is etymologically related to an Arabic word that means "be under, submissive."

In only 14 of its 82 uses are the poor specified in the context (but note the wide range of its meanings). As a matter of fact, *'anah* is the very first word we find in the Bible to express oppression. In the story of the covenant with Abraham, Yahweh says to the patriarch:

Know of a surety that your descendants will be immigrants in a land that is not theirs, and will be slaves there, and they will be oppressed *('anah)* for four hundred years . . . and afterward they will come out [liberation] with great possessions [Gen. 15:13].

Possible implications for biblical sexual ethics structured around oppression and liberation remain largely unexplored. On fasting as "oppressing the soul," see chapter 2, note 1, below. According to this text, the chosen people's experience, like that of Joseph, prefigures Christ's humiliation and exaltation. The order is typical: first immigrants without land (a vulnerable situation); later enslaved; and consequently oppressed, loaded down like beasts of burden.[19]

In view of the covenantal structure evident in many of the theological perspectives of the Old Testament, it is important to note that *liberation from oppression is one of the fundamental provisions* (along with land and posterity ["seed"]) *of the Abrahamic covenant.* Inasmuch as Paul in the New Testament singles out this Abrahamic covenant as the eternal "saving" covenant (Gal. 3–4), this fact must affect our whole understanding of "salvation" as integral liberation.

'Anah is also, appropriately, the first word used in Exodus to describe the oppression suffered by Abraham's descendants:

> Therefore they set taskmasters over them to oppress *('anah)* them with heavy burdens. . . . But the more they were oppressed *('anah),* the more they multiplied and the more they spread abroad [Exod. 1:11, 12].

The introductory genealogy (Exod. 1:1–7), indicating Israel's "roots," has made clear that the nation is not poor because of racial inferiority or "under-development." These poor slaves are in fact descendants of the great patriarchs of Genesis. They have become poor because a great empire has begun to oppress them. The only sin indicated is the sin of their oppressors.

The paradigmatic function of this exodus experience (oppression/liberation) begins to operate already in that ancient collection of laws known as the Book of the Covenant (Exod. 20:22–23:33):

> You shall not wrong *(yanah)* an immigrant or oppress *(lahats)* him, for you were immigrants in the land of Egypt. You shall not oppress *('anah)* any widow or orphan. If you oppress *('anah)* them and they cry out to me, I will surely hear their outcry; and my wrath will burn, and I will kill you with the sword, and your wives shall become widows and your children fatherless (22:21–24).

Significantly, there are three words for oppression in this brief passage: *yanah, lahats,* and *'anah,* with *'anah* appearing twice. The relationship between poverty and oppression is made clear by the three common classes of poor and weak persons mentioned: immigrants, widows, and orphans. We should notice that *only here* in the entire Book of the Covenant does God's *wrath* threaten the guilty parties in their punishment. Other crimes are punishable by death, but only when the poor suffer oppression does God declare that the death penalty definitely expresses his wrath. (We may compare this to Jesus' teaching about hell in the parable of the final judgment, Matt. 25:31–46.) In fact, when God forbids oppression of the poor in the Book of the Covenant, it is the *first time* the Scriptures explicitly affirm that God becomes angry. Liberal theologies commonly evade biblical teaching on God's wrath; but conservatives have overlooked the fact that this wrath is primarily manifested against injustice and oppression of the poor (see Rom. 1:18).[20]

Psalm 94 also shows us another clear link between oppression and poverty:

> They pulverize with oppression *(daka')* thy people, O Lord,
>   and humiliatingly oppress *('anah)* thy heritage.
> They slay the widow and the sojourner,
>   and murder the fatherless [94:5–6].

The two words for oppression appear in a parallelism that underlies both the physical and psychological effects of oppression. As in other texts, the poor are depicted concretely as the three defenseless classes of the ancient social order: immigrants, widows, and orphans.

Before turning to another crucial text that emphasizes the link between oppression and poverty in biblical theology, we must first note an important linguistic fact that bears on our study. According to the lexicons, two common Old Testament words for "poor" come from the verb *'anah*—namely, *'anaw* ("poor, humble, meek") and *'ani* ("oppressed, poor, humble").[21] Thus both etymology and the usage pattern of these three words signal the intrinsic relationship between oppression and poverty in Hebrew thought.

Thus we may better understand Deuteronomy 26:5–10, which, since Gerhard von Rad, modern studies have referred to as a kind of Old Testament "Apostles' Creed." At every celebration of the Feast of the First Fruits (similar to Thanksgiving Day in the U.S.A. and Canada), the Israelites confessed:

> A wandering Aramean was my father; and he went down into Egypt and sojourned there, few in number; and there he became a nation, great, mighty, and populous. And the Egyptians treated us harshly, and oppressed *('anah)* us, and laid upon us hard bondage.
>
> Then we cried to the Lord the God of our fathers, and the Lord heard our voice, and saw our poverty *('ani),* our toil, and our oppression *(lahats)*; and the Lord brought us out of Egypt with a mighty hand and an outstretched arm, with great terror, with signs and wonders; and he brought us into this place and gave us this land, a land flowing with milk and honey [Deut. 26:5–9].

This "Apostles' Creed" well sums up the fundamental role that oppression plays in Old Testament theology. Later, when Israel had become rich (Deut. 8:17, 18), God never let it forget either its solidarity with its oppressed ancestors or the liberation that God had given it because of his love. In individual cases the Old Testament lists many possible causes of poverty. Nevertheless, oppression was the only cause that "orthodox believers" had to affirm confessionally each year. Awareness of that cause as a "fundamental doctrine" was basic for anyone who belonged to God's people. It was thus impossible to suppose that poverty was basically the result of the sins of the poor or some kind of mental or racial inferiority or of "underdevelopment." To be a "fundamentalist" in Israel you had to recognize that poverty is fundamentally rooted in oppression—and that Yahweh's purpose in history is liberation.

§8. Oppression Expresses Enmity—"*tsar*, "*tsarar*,

"*Tsar*. In the study of the noun "*tsar* the lexicons and translations present us with a strange combination of facts.[22] "*Tsar* occurs 70 times in the Old

Testament and is related etymologically to words signifying "hostility." It is derived from the verb "*tsarar* ("be hostile, be in conflict"). However, Holladay gives as its first definition "oppressor," following Koehler (German: *Bedrängner*). Holladay's other definitions are "adversary" and "enemy." The English renderings in Koehler follow BDB (Brown-Driver-Briggs) and give only "adversary" and "foe," leaving *Bedrängner* without an English equivalent. Despite the express preference of both Koehler and Holladay for the definition "oppressor," I cannot find a single instance where modern translations so render this noun. However, inasmuch as "*tsar* most commonly (21 times) parallels "enemy" *('oyeb),* it would appear that usage supports the etymological sense ("hostility") and the lexicons should have given "adversary" and "foe" as the primary definitions.

On the other hand, "oppressor" should not be eliminated as a legitimate translation of "*tsar* (as in BDB), because historically and contextually Israel's foes commonly were the surrounding oppressor empires. And in fact "*tsar* (and *'oyeb,* "enemy") often occur in relationship with other basic vocabulary for oppression as well as poverty.

The link with oppression is evident in Psalm 74:

> How long, O God, will the oppressor foe ("*tsar)* mock?
> Shall the enemy *('oyeb)* revile your name forever? [v. 10].

However, verse 8 says of the same invading Babylonians: "They said in their hearts, 'we will oppress *(ynh)* them completely.' " And the psalm concludes with the plea:

> Do not hand over the life of your doves to wild beasts;
>   do not forget the lives of your poor *('ani)* forever.
> Have regard for your covenant [Gen. 15]
>   because haunts of violence *(hamas)* fill
>   the dark places of the land.
> Do not let the oppressed *(dak)* retreat in disgrace;
>   may the poor *('ani)* and needy *('ebyon)* praise your name [74:19-21].

However, if "oppressor" be accepted as a legitimate (if not preferable) translation of "*tsar* in such texts as Psalm 74, many other familiar contexts may best be understood in that light. For instance:

> Yahweh is my light and my liberation
>   whom shall I fear. . . .
> When evil men advance against me to devour my flesh,
>   my oppressors ("*tsar)* and enemies *('oyeb),*
>   They will stumble and fall.
> Teach me your way, O Yahweh;
>   lead me in a straight path because of my oppressors [NIV;
>   Heb. *shrr*].

Do not give me up to the greed of my oppressors (^{II}*tsar)*
for false witnesses have risen against me
and breathe out violence *(ḥamas)* [Ps. 27:1a, 2, 11–12].

The NIV is notable here: it translates Hebrew *shrr* "oppressors," contrary to
the lexicons ("enemy," "foe," 5 or 6 times, total), but ^{II}*tsar* is translated
"foes," when both Holladay and Koehler give "oppressor" as the first
definition.

In addition to frequent links with basic roots for oppression, poverty is
commonly indicated in the context with ^{II}*tsar.* Thus, Zechariah refers to the
frustration and poverty of the postexilic remnant when the temple foundation
was laid:

Before those days there were no wages for man nor wages for beast. No
one could go about his business safely because of the oppressor (^{II}*tsar)*
[8:10].

In all, poverty is closely linked to ^{II}*tsar* in six instances (Zech. 8:10; Ps.
119:157; 136:24; Lam. 1:7 [twice], 10).

^{II}*Tsarar.* Strangely, though Holladay and Koehler give "oppressor" as the
first definition of the noun ^{II}*tsar,* they do not give "oppress" as a possible
definition of the related verb ^{II}*tsarar* ("be hostile toward, be in a state of
conflict with"). Translations and commentaries wisely often go beyond the
lexicons, particularly in contexts that link ^{II}*tsarar* with poverty. Thus NIV
translates the verb ^{II}*tsarar* "oppress" four times:

When you go into battle in your own land against an enemy [^{II}*tsar* =
oppressor] who is oppressing (^{II}*tsarar)* you, sound a blast on the
trumpets [Num. 10:9; liberation from a powerful, invading oppressor is
to be heralded by the trumpet blast (cf. the Jubilee and New Testament
references to Jesus' Second Coming)].
    You oppress (^{II}*tsarar)* the righteous and take bribes and you deprive
the poor *('ebyon)* of justice in the courts [Amos 5:12].

The RSV "afflict" and NEB "persecute" (!) are obviously inferior to the NIV
here.

Especially significant is the testimony in Psalm 129 that Israel's entire
history as a nation is a history of oppression (the presupposition to salvation
or liberation history):

They [Egypt] have greatly oppressed (^{II}*tsarar)* me from my youth
    let Israel say—
They have greatly oppressed (^{II}*tsarar)* me from my youth
    [Ps. 129:1–2].

In these cases NIV goes beyond lexical definitions. But in most of the 26
occurrences of ^{II}*tsarar* in the Old Testament, "oppress" in the sense of "show

hostility by oppression'' is at least as satisfactory a translation as is "be
hostile," because the hostility Israel primarily experienced was from powerful,
unjust oppressors.

Thus in Psalm 23 we might just as well translate:

> You prepare a table before me [hunger]
> in the presence of my oppressors ("*tsarar;* NIV, "enemies"") [23:5a].

The psalm expresses the confidence of the oppressed poor that Yahweh, the
liberator of the exodus, will supply his essential needs (vv. 1–2), guide him in
paths of justice (v. 3) and liberation from threatened death (v. 4). Instead of
Pharaoh's pursuing cavalry, he looks back to discover Yahweh's covenanted
goodness and mercy following him (v. 6; cf. Gen. 15).

Most often "*tsarar* parallels terms for enemies (*'oyeb,* etc.). However, it is
also used with other terms for oppression in three contexts: Num. 10:9 ("*tsar)*;
Ps. 42:11 *(lahats);* and 143:12 *(dc',* 3).

In addition to Amos 5:12 (cited above) the link with poverty is especially
strong in Ps. 69:20[19] and 74:23 (total, with Amos, 3 times; total with the
noun "*tsar,* 9 times).

§9. Oppression Impoverishes—¹*tsarar,* ¹*tsar,* ¹*tsarah*

¹*Tsarar.* The verb ¹*tsarar* occurs 46 times in the Old Testament.[23] Etymologically it is related to nouns meaning "rope" and "bridle" and to an Arabic
verb meaning "tie." Holladay gives us a transitive meaning, "tie up," and as
basic definitions of the qal intransitive "be narrow, cramped, hampered,
impeded." However, he also gives us a third definition, "be hard pressed,
in distress" and as a fourth possibility "be oppressed, afflicted" (also the
hifil, "oppress, afflict"). The English renderings in Koehler do not mention
oppression, but in the German the fourth definition, *bedrückt,* might well be
rendered "oppressed" as in Holladay.

Often the historical and literary context confirms that "oppress" may be the
primary nuance of ¹*tsarar.* Thus in Psalm 106 we read:

> Their enemies oppressed *(lhts)* them
> and subjected them to their power [NIV, v. 42].

But then in verse 44:

> But [Yahweh] took note of their oppression (¹*tsarar;* NIV, "distress")
> when he heard their cry.

The NIV renders this verb "oppress" at least once (Neh. 9:27).
The link with poverty is particularly explicit in Isaiah (25:4):

You have been a refuge for the poor *(dal)*
   a refuge to the needy *('ebyon)* in his oppression (*'tsarar;* NIV,
"distress").

Poverty is directly related to *'tsarar* 5 times (Judg. 2:15; Ps. 31:108; 107:6, 13).

'Tsar. The masculine noun *'tsar,* derived from the verb *'tsarar* ("tie up, be narrow, cramped"), occurs some 17 times in the Old Testament. In four texts the meaning is literally "narrowness." In the other 13 uses the lexicons suggest such definitions as "distress, want, need" (Koehler, German: *Not*). The historical and literary contexts commonly suggest a nuance of "poverty caused by oppression." Thus Isaiah 30:20, referring to seige or prison conditions, might well be translated:

Although Yahweh gives you the bread of oppression *(laḥats)*
   and the water of oppression-caused poverty *('tsar)*
your teachers will be hidden no more.

Also in Psalm 119 we find *'tsar* linked directly with another basic term for oppression:

Need *('tsar)* and oppression *(matsoq)* overtook me,
   but your commandments are my delight [v. 143].

We do not find *'tsar* directly linked to other basic Hebrew vocabulary for poverty, but the meaning of the word itself causes this nuance ("want, need"). In this respect it resembles *'ani,* which the lexicons define both as "poor" and "oppressed" (see §7, above, under *'anah*).

'Tsarah. *'Tsarah* is a feminine noun derived, like *'tsar* (m.), from the verb *'tsarar* ("be narrow"). It is much more common (69 times) than *'tsar* (17 times), its masculine counterpart. Koehler and Holladay give only one definition: "distress" (KB², German: *Not,* "need"). The BDB lexicon prefers "straits," reflecting more closely the etymology of the verb ("be narrow"). However, in the vast majority of its 69 uses in the Old Testament, "oppression" would be at least as suitable a translation: the word mainly describes the kind of "straits" or "distress" experienced by Israel, as a poor, weak nation struggling against powerful, unjust empires (Egypt, Assyria, Babylonia, etc.). Thus in Nehemiah's prayer he refers to Israel's oppression and liberation in the time of the judges:

So you handed them [Israel] over to their enemies [*"tsar* = oppressors] who oppressed [*'tsarar]* them. But when they were oppressed [*'tsarah:* literally, "in the time of their oppression"] they cried out to you [9:27a, NIV].

The prayer concludes:

> But see, we are slaves today, slaves in the land you gave our forefathers
> so they could eat its fruit and the other good things it produces. Because
> of our sins, its abundant harvest goes to the kings you have placed over
> us. They rule over our bodies and our cattle as they please. We are in
> great distress ['*tsarah* = oppression; 9:36–37, NIV].

It is notable here that NIV goes beyond the lexicons and translates '*tsarah* as
"oppressed" in 9:27. The context in 9:37 would make "oppression" at least as
suitable a translation as the vague and colorless "distress," given the double
reference to "slaves," and to rapacious, tyrannical kings. Obviously Nehemiah views Israel as reliving the exodus oppression experiences and hopes for
a similar miraculous liberation.

As the BDB lexicon indicates, a peculiarity of '*tsarah* is its frequent use in
temporal expressions: in a "day" *(yom)* of *tsarah* (15 times) and in a "time"
('et) of *tsarah* (8 times). This usage, along with frequent contextual references
(Jeremiah) to a woman's travail in childbirth, often give the word a nuance of
crisis, an urgent condition that must result in liberation or death. Thus in
Jeremiah 30:7 the oft-cited reference to the "time *('et)* of Jacob's trouble
('*tsarah)*" is actually a reference to imperial Babylonian oppression (cf. Dan.
12:1). Occasionally '*tsarah* is used with more explicit terms for oppression: Isa.
8:22, *tsuqah* and, v. 23, *mutsaq;* 30:6, *tsuqah;* Zeph. 1:15, *metsuqah;* Ps. 34:
18, *dc',* v. 19; Prov. 1:27, *tsuqah.*

Poverty is commonly suggested in the general historical or literary context
and a direct link between *tsarah* and poverty is explicit five times: Ps. 27:27
('*ani,* vv. 16, 18); 31:8 *('ani);* 86:7 ('*ani* and '*ebyon,* v. 1); Isa. 8:22 ("hungry,"
v. 21).

Thus '*tsarar* and its cognates occur a total of 132 times, with poverty indicated in the context 10 times.

§10. Oppression Beseiges (Eschatological)—*tsuq* and Cognates

The verb *tsuq* occurs 11 times in the Old Testament and is related to an
Akkadian root meaning "narrow."[24] It is defined by Holladay and Koehler as
"oppress" (German: *bedrängen*) or "bring into straits." This verb has five
related cognates: the nouns *tsoq,* "oppression" (once); *tsuqah,* "oppression,
distress" (3 times); *mutsaq,* "oppression, hardship" (3 times); *matsoq,*
"hardship" (6 times); and "*metsuqah,* "oppression" (7 times). Most often
tsuq and its cognates occur in contexts describing seige conditions in connection with a similar root *tswr,* "beseige," and its related noun *matsor,*
"oppression, stress" (see below, chap. 2). In eschatological contexts the "last
days" of a city or people become associated with the last days of the great
tribulation-oppression preceding the decisive divine intervention.

Thus in Deuteronomy 28:53, 55, 57 the verb *tsuq* occurs together with the nouns *matsoq* and *matsor* three times to describe the terrible conditions during the seige-oppression *(matsor)* of Jerusalem (587 B.C.) preceding the Babylonian exile. Seige conditions as a type of oppression are similarly indicated in two uses of the verb in Isaiah, perhaps with reference to Sennacherib's invasion and seige in 701 B.C. (29:2, 7, Jerusalem called "Ariel"). Later, in Isaiah, the word again occurs twice (in one verse, 51:13) related to the "fury" *(hemah)* of the Babylonian oppressor.

The rare nouns *tsuqah* and *mutsaq* occur together with three other words lexically defined as "oppression" in Isaiah 8:21–9:4[5] (see comments above under *nagas,* §3). Our translations utterly fail to make clear the heavy stress on oppression in this fundamental messianic text, concluding with the birth announcement of 9:5[6]: "For unto us a child is born. . . ." The historical background refers to the expansion of the cruel Assyrian empire, which, from 734 to 32 B.C., under Tiglath Pilesar, conquered and annexed the northern and eastern areas of the Northern Kingdom (New Testament Galilee). Faced with cruel invaders and terrifying seige conditions, the Israelites (like Saul at Gilboa) were tempted to turn from the torah and the prophets to spiritism, mediums, witches (8:19–20). The five lexically defined references to oppression then follow:

> Oppressed *(qshh)* and hungry they will roam through the land [8:21].
> Then they will look toward the earth and see only oppression (*'tsarah)*
>   and darkness and gloom of oppression *(tsuqah)* [8:22].
> Nevertheless there will be no more gloom for those who were oppressed
>   *(mutsaq)* [8:23 (9:1)],
> For as in the day of Midian's defeat you have shattered the yoke that
>   burdens them, the bar across their shoulders, the rod of the one
>   oppressing *(nagas)* them [9:3(4)].

In addition to the five explicit words defined by the lexicons as "oppression," we have oppression symbolized by a yoke and bar in 9:3[4] and also six times by darkness, gloom, and the shadow of death (8:22–23; 9:1[2]). The decisive liberation inaugurated by the Messiah's birth is then symbolized by great light, dawn, and glory (8:20, 23; 9:1[2]). The people's response to liberation is one of supreme joy, compared to the harvest time (9:3a[4a]) and celebration of a military victory such as Gideon's against the powerful Midianites (9:3b[4b]).

Concerning the oppression detailed in 9:4, Young observes:

> Israel was like an animal [*nagas!*] of toil over whose neck a heavy
> wooden bar lay. . . . As every beast of burden and toil is beaten with a
> rod, so Israel also had a rod with which it was beaten on the neck or
> shoulder. There was also, as in Egypt, an oppressor who used a staff to
> strike the beast. The oppressor was the Assyrian enemy.[25]

Young then comments on the liberation from oppression to be inaugurated by the child's *birth* (not just the second coming!):

> Salvation in its widest sense ["integral liberation?"] had shined upon these people; a complete reversal of their condition had occurred.[26]

Regarding the liberating effects that flow from the child's birth, Young concludes:

> When the Son appears in life with the attributes here assigned to Him, then the kingdom will be founded and established. The kingdom of the Son *continually progresses.* Justice and righteousness are its foundation; *oppression and injustice* have no part in its progress and *growth* [italics added].[27]

In the words of a New Testament writer, God *is* (liberating) *light;* moreover "the darkness is passing and the true light is already shining" (1 John 1:5; 2:8).

Another link with the New Testament perspective on oppression and liberation may be seen in Psalm 107. Traditional interpretations of the psalm are radically transformed when we recognize that it is structured around four types of oppression (*metsuqah* and *tsar,* vv. 6, 13, 19, 18) as experienced by the exiles. Poverty is clearly indicated in the first context (vv. 5, 9; hunger and thirst of exiles). Also in the second context the prisoners are viewed as locked ("iron fetters") into their poverty (*'ani,* v. 10; cf. *'otser,* v. 39). And as in Isaiah, whereas darkness symbolized their oppression, liberation leads to light and life (v. 14). However, physical sickness is then viewed as a consequence of oppression in verses 18–20, as is a storm at sea (vv. 28–29; cf. Deut. 28:68). In these latter instances we are moving toward the broader New Testament view of oppression as including sickness and a diabolical dimension. The demonic dimension expresses itself through sickness (Acts 10:38; see chap. 3, below) and other elements of creation (the storm "rebuked" by Jesus, in Mark 5:39). Each stanza of the psalm concludes with praise to God for being faithful *(ḥesed)* to his covenant promises to Abraham (Gen. 15, liberation from oppression).

Psalm 25 also uses *metsuqah* (v. 17) in a context marked by frequent references to poverty (*'ani,* 16b, 18a; *'anawim,* 9ab), another term for oppression (*tsar,* 17a, 23b), violence (*ḥamas,* 19b and—in contrast—liberation (*ysh',* 5b; *yts',* 17b; *ntsl,* 20a; *pdh,* 22a). This psalm on divine guidance thus recalls the place of guidance as normatively *following* the liberation experience in the exodus paradigm (the pillar of cloud and fire; the decalogue of Exod. 20; detailed stipulations of the Book of the Covenant, Exod. 21–23). Laws for the amelioration of the plight of the poor thus are not given to Moses—much less to the pharaoh—during the oppression in Egypt. They are given as guidance for a "postrevolutionary" situation—to liberated slaves en route to their promised land.

Finally we should note how common seige associations of *metsuqah* acquire eschatological significance. Zephaniah describes the great Day of the Lord as a day of "wrath, adversity *(tsarah)*" and "oppression *(metsuqah)*" as well as "darkness and gloom . . . clouds and thick darkness" (1:15), and marked by invasion and seige (vv. 16 ff.). Similarly in Daniel's controversial prophecy of the 70 weeks we read: "The street shall be built again and the wall even in times of oppression *(tsoq)*"; (9:25). The noun *tsoq* employed for oppression occurs only here in the Old Testament. Recent interpreters have pointed to the Jubilee pattern (7 times 7; Lev. 25:8 ff.) to explain the division of the number (7 sevens and 62 sevens). However the details of the prophecy be interpreted, the relationship between times of oppression *(tsoq)* and the Jubilee-type liberation must be significant factors—and of much greater importance than the endless speculation about chronology.[28]

In summary we may say that words signifying oppression from the *tsuq* family occur 31 times, with poverty indicated in the context 14 times. The seige contexts (last days of a city) prepare us for the eschatological references to the last days in Daniel and Zephaniah (Day of the Lord). With this we may compare the reference to the "time of Jacob's oppression *(tsarah)*" in Jeremiah 30:7 and the great tribulation-oppression *(thlīpsis)* in Revelation (see below, chap. 3).[29]

Chapter 2

Other Old Testament Indices

TEN LESS FREQUENT HEBREW ROOTS
FOR "OPPRESSION"

In addition to the ten basic roots for oppression studied above, some ten other Hebrew roots of less frequent occurrence are also translated "oppress/oppression" (German: *Bedrängnis*) in the Hebrew lexicons. Usually this meaning is obscured in our common translations. Although the total number of occurrences of these roots is small (some occur only once), often their literal sense illumines contexts of theological importance in a significant way.

Below are listed the ten less frequent roots in alphabetical order. I shall then illustrate briefly, with reference to their theological significance, some of the contexts where they occur. For details regarding etymologies, additional possible meanings, and conjectural readings (cj.), the reader may consult the lexicons of Koehler (KB²) and Holladay (Hol.). Texts referring to poverty are italicized.

1) *Dḥq* (twice): Joel 2:8 (with *lḥts*); *Judg. 2:18*; Mic. 7:11 cj.; Zeph. 2:2. KB², p. 207; Hol., p. 70.

2) *Zw'* (3 times): *Hab. 2:7;* Ecclus. 12:3; Esther 5:9. KB², p. 253; Hol., p. 87.

3) *Ḥamots* (twice): *Isa. 1:17;* 16:4. ᴵᴵ*ḥmts* (once): Ps. 71:4; cf. Isa. 16:4. KB², pp. 310, 312; Hol., pp. 108 f.

4) *Kff* (4 times): Isa. 58:5; *Ps. 57:7;* 145:14; *146:8.* KB², p. 451; Hol., p. 163.

5) ᴵ*Matsor* (6 times): *Deut. 28:53, 55, 57; Jer. 10:17, 19:9;* Ps. 31:22; Ps. 32:6 cj.; 66:11. KB², p. 556; Hol., p. 211. Holladay considers Koehler's ᴵᴵ*matsor* ("seige") the same word.

6) *'awwatah* (once): Lam. 3:59. Cf. the verb *'wth* ("make crooked, pervert"). KB², p. 692; Hol., p. 269.

26

7) *'otser* and *'etser* (4 times): Judg. 18:7; *Isa. 53:8; Ps. 107:39;* Prov. 30:16. KB², p. 729; Hol., p. 281.

8) *Qshh* (once): *Isa. 8:21.* See our discussion of the context under *tsuq,* chapter 1, §10, above. KB², p. 859; Hol., p. 326.

9) *Tolal* (once): Ps. 137:3. KB², p. 1021; Hol., p. 387.

10) *Tōk* (4 times): *Ps. 10:7;* 55:12; *72:14; Prov. 29:13.* Cf. Ps. 90:11; Jer. 9:5. KB², p. 1028; Hol., p. 390.

kff

Of the ten less frequent Hebrew roots lexically defined as "oppress/ oppression," perhaps the most important theologically is *kff,* most often translated "bow down." Thus in Psalm 146 we have the affirmation:

> Yahweh is opening [the eyes of] the blind;
> Yahweh is raising up those who are oppressed-bowed down *(kff)*
> [v. 8b].

Oppression, poverty, and liberation are particularly prominent in the context. Thus in a series of participles stressing Yahweh's continuous and characteristic activities, he is described as one:

> Who is keeping truth [fulfilling promises] forever,
> Who is doing just judgments for the oppressed *('ashuqim)* [6b-7a].

Undoubtedly this is an allusion to the exodus paradigm stressing fulfillment of the covenant promises to Abraham (Gen. 15: seed, liberation from oppression, land, prosperity). The link between oppression and poverty becomes clearer in verse 7b:

> Who is giving bread to the hungry;
> Yahweh is loosing the prisoner.

Then, following the reference to the oppressed as bowed down (*kff,* 8b), the psalmist refers to Yahweh's special protection of the classic three oppressed classes: immigrants, orphans, and widows (v. 9). The psalm thus emphasizes how the power of the Creator himself (v. 6a) is viewed as continually and characteristically (9 participles) at work in history to repeat the exodus paradigm of liberation. In such a context the "bowed down" *(kff)* obviously refers primarily to the oppressed, overloaded with heavy labor and with the resulting physical condition that commonly results (cf. Luke 13:11).

In Psalm 145 the exodus paradigm (alluded to in the "bowed down") is explicitly universalized:

Yahweh is sustaining all who are falling down
and raising up all who are bowed down *(kff)* [v. 14; cf. 103:6–7].

Isaiah 58 (see chap. 6, below) uses *kff* in parallelism with *'nh,* one of the
basic Hebrew roots for oppression (chap. 1, §7, above).

Is this the kind of fast *(tsom)* I choose,
only a day for a man to oppress *('nh)* his soul,
to bow down *(kff)* his head like a bulrush . . .? [v. 5].

The context refers repeatedly to the poor (v. 7b), the oppressed (*rtsts,* v. 6b;
'nh, v. 10b), and the need for a decisive Jubilee-type liberation (v. 6de; Luke
4:19; see chap 6 and 7, below).

We should note, too, that according to Hebrew thought a "fast" *(tsom)* is
conceived of as a time when one literally "oppresses" *('nh)* one's soul
(*nephesh,* "life") by making it go hungry like the poor. Fasting is thus an act
of identification and solidarity with the poor, recalling acts of liberation (Isa.
58:6) such as the Jubilee (Lev. 25), which was inaugurated by Israel's only
legal fast day. Jesus' 40-day fast (Luke 4:2), before proclaiming his good news
to the poor and liberation for the oppressed (Luke 4:18–19), should be
understood against this background. Fasting in the Bible is never just negative
oriental "asceticism" but a positive act of solidarity with the poor and needy
and renewed commitment to their liberation—a repetition of the exodus
paradigm. Although many Protestants oscillate between church dinners and
Weight Watchers, and some Catholics and Pentecostals call for a return to
fasting as a meritorious ascetic act, the biblical concept of fasting continues to
call us to a profounder and more positive practice of this ancient discipline—in
terms of oppression and liberation.[1]

tōk

Tōk occurs four times in the Old Testament, always in poetic passages.
Etymologically *tōk* is related to an Arabic verb meaning "tread on." The
lexicons define it as "oppression" or, in the plural, when used with *'ish,*
"man," (e.g., Prov. 29:13), as "tyrant." It describes the kind of oppression
that tyrannizes. Twice (Ps. 55:12; 10:7) it is associated with lies
(propaganda?).

Although *tōk* is not a common word, it gives us even more linguistic
evidence in our study of the link between oppression and poverty in the Old
Testament. In two of the four uses, the poor are mentioned in the immediate
context (Ps. 72:14; Prov. 29:13) and in the third use (Ps. 10:7) they are
mentioned earlier. (See our reference to this psalm under *daka'* and *tsuq,*
chap. 1, §§6 and 10, above.)

Theologically the most important text in this group is Proverbs 29:13:

A poor man and his oppressor *(tōk)* exist side by side,
Yahweh illumines the eyes of them both.

The parallelism reminds us of the Bible's realism concerning the existence of social classes and the tensions among them: the poor are the oppressed and God's sovereign rule sets the bounds within which human injustice, oppression, and sin may play only a limited part. Thus, to counteract any tendency of tyrants and oppressors to deify themselves, the Scriptures erect a dike of solemn warnings: oppressors and the poor share a common origin (Prov. 22:20) and common blessings (29:13), and are destined for a common end (Job 3:19).[2] This perspective gives the lie to any idea of social or racial superiority. Such texts seek to humble the oppressor and to encourage the poor with reminders of their essential dignity as God's image bearers. The strong witness to God's just order, which such texts give, helps prepare the soil for the decisive exoduslike events.

'otser and *'etser*

'Otser occurs three times in the Old Testament and *'etser* only once. Koehler defines both as "oppression." The contexts in two cases (Isa. 53:8 and Ps. 107:39) suggest the oppression that the poor suffer in the courts. Unjust judges and bribed officials loom large in the Bible, as in life today, especially among the collaborating oligarchies in Third World countries. Acts 8:33 quotes Isaiah 53:8 but follows the LXX, which renders it "humiliation."

tolal

The shocking imprecations of Psalm 137 ("By the rivers of Babylon") are better understood when we recognize the context of oppression indicated by *tolal,* a word occurring only here in the Hebrew Bible:

Because there our captors asked us the words of a song,
and our oppressors *(tolal)* gladness [v. 3a].

Koehler (p. 1021) here resorts to textual emendation. But Holladay prefers to translate "oppressors" (p. 387). H. J. Kraus derives the word from the hifil (causative) root of *yll*—literally, "to make howl" (cf. NIV, "tormentors").[3] This fits well with the parallel expression to "our captors/guards" (v. 3a) and with the general context ("there we wept," v. 1b). The exiles' guards demand a "song" not from sincere appreciation of the music or pious interest in the truth of Israel's faith, but as a means of torment. The reference to oppression *(tolal)* underlines the political significance of the Israelites' gesture, which Derek Kidner calls "a fine stubbornness."[4] The Israelite exiles act in solidarity with a gesture of passive defiance to their oppressors. The hanging of their harps on the willows is a kind of "strike" in response to the torment of the oppressors (cf. the midwives in Exod. 1).

The shocking imprecation at the psalm's conclusion may impress us as failing to attain the heights of forgiving love attested in the Old as well as the New Testament. But forgiveness must be conditioned upon sincere repentance (of which the oppressors here show no evidence). And a desperate prayer for *divine* judgment (instead of overt vengeance) is still more than most Christians manage even in circumstances only remotely similar. Thus in light of the context (oppression) the imprecatory prayer must be understood as a desperate plea for liberation. In the face of obdurate, cruel oppressors, liberation may come only when God sees fit to judge and overthrow them.

ḥamots

In addition to Psalms, Isaiah is particularly noteworthy for the use of rarer terms for oppression at key points. Thus in Isaiah 1:17 we have the famous exhortation:

> Cease to do evil;
> Learn to do good;
> Seek justice *(mishpat)*
> Reprove *('shr)* the oppressor *(ḥamots)*
> Give the orphan his rights *(shft);*
> Plead the case of the widow.

Koehler (p. 310) and Holladay (p. 108) agree in translating *ḥamots* actively as "the oppressor" (cf. NIV passive, "encourage the oppressed"). The noun occurs only here in the Old Testament. The passive (weaker) sense preferred by NIV (cf. NEB, "champion the oppressed") requires a small vocalic change in the Hebrew text (*ḥamuts* instead of *ḥamots*).

E. J. Young, following Delitzsch, rejects the emendation as unnecessary.[5] The accompanying verb *('shr)* is defined by Koehler (p. 95) as "reprove," a favorite wisdom term and also popular with Isaiah. As Young says, the reproving or setting right of the oppressor "may be accomplished either by bonds or by other punishment and the idea of constraint is present." He adds that the "first step" in pursuing justice is "the restraining of oppression, so that it must go the straight way."[6] But then after properly expounding what the text clearly says about the need to reprove and even forcibly constrain and punish oppressors, Young inconsistently concludes: "Such social injustice, however, could only [!] be corrected by a change of heart upon the part of individuals."[7] With that approach Israel should still be enslaved in Egypt praying for the pharaoh to be converted! Isaiah, of course, is a superb evangelist. But his "good news for the poor" also involves fearless proclamation of bad news for unrepentant oppressors. "Learning to do good" involves *reproving* the oppressors and serving *justice*—not just charity—for the oppressed poor. Did not the prejudices of pietism so often suffocate sound exegesis and exposition of the Scriptures, Isaiah might have more worthy imitators today!

The ten less frequent Hebrew roots for oppression occur a total of 30 times (15 with the poor) in contexts that are often theologically important.

THE BROADER SEMANTIC FIELD FOR "OPPRESSION"

In addition to the twenty Hebrew roots lexically defined in some form as "oppress/oppression/oppressor," the Old Testament of course includes many other terms that should be included in the broader semantic field. Commentaries and translations occasionally opt for the nuance of oppression in specific contexts, and the link with poverty is often apparent. Evidence for the oppression-poverty link is greatly increased when we start from the terms for "poor/poverty" and look for contextual evidence for oppression, which may be indicated by the following more general terms as well as the twenty Hebrew roots studied above. We have not included Aramaic vocabulary from Daniel, but see *blh* "wear down" (7:25; cf. 1 Chr. 17:9, Hol., pp. 399, 340).

1) *Shōd* (20 times): KB², p. 949; Hol., p. 361. Commonly defined as "destruction, devastation," *shōd* is linked to the poor in Psalm 12:6 and translated "oppression" in the NIV: " 'Because of the oppression *(shōd)* of the weak *('aniyiym)* and the groaning of the needy *('ebyonim)* I will now arise,' says the Lord." RSV translates *shōd* here "despoiled"; NEB, "ruin"; AB, "sobs."

2) *Gzl,* "take away by force, rob": KB², pp. 177 f.; Hol., p. 58. Contextually *gzl* often indicates a mechanism of oppression.

3) *'sr,* "imprison," and *'asir,* "prisoner": KB², pp. 73 f.; Hol., p. 23. Most imprisonment was for debt and exile, not crime, and even the latter often involved false accusations (Joseph), a common mechanism of oppression.

4) *Ygh,* "afflict, grieve, torment": KB², p. 361; Hol., p. 127. Of its total 8 occurrences, 5 are in Lamentations (1:4, 5, 12; 3:32, 33), where it might well be rendered "grievously oppress," etc.

5) *Medushah* (once), "downtrodden": KB², p. 498; Hol., p. 183. "O my people crushed *(medushah)* on the threshing floor" (Isa. 21:10, NIV).

6) *'aqah* (once), "pressure": KB², p. 730; Hol., p. 281. Psalm 55:4[3] is translated in the RSV: "I am distraught by the noise of the enemy *('oyeb)* because of the oppression *('aqah)* of the wicked *(rasha')*. José P. Miranda points out that the wicked *(rasha';* plural, *resha'im)* in the psalms is basically a reference to oppressors of the poor. He argues: "Given the abundance of items offered us by the Psalter for understanding who the *resha'im* are, I think we are at the Archimedean point of our interpretation of the Psalter."[8]

7) *'Arits,* "master, violent, tyrant": KB², p. 735; Hol., p. 285. Especially notable is the use in Isaiah 29, where references to the *'anawim* ("oppressed-humble-poor") and *'ebyon* ("poor, needy") are followed by the promise that "the ruthless (*'arits,* "oppressor") will vanish" (NIV).

8) *'R'h,* "feed, graze, pasture": KB², pp. 898 f.; Hol., p. 342. Occasionally it becomes a metaphor for oppression and violence ("cannibalism") against the poor, as in Job 24:21 (NIV, "prey . . . on the widow"); cf. 6:23; Micah 3:1–3.

The metaphorical language for oppression, of course, would be a large study in itself. And the number of texts relating oppression to poverty would be greatly increased by taking into account the links between the vocabulary for the poor and metaphorical language for oppression. Thus, in Amos we have only two basic roots for oppression linked to the poor: *'shq* with *dal* (4:1b), and *rtsts* with *'ebyon* (4:1c); but compare the linkage of *tsrr* with *tsadiq,* "the just" (5:12c). However, we have seven additional instances where Amos uses metaphorical language for oppression and description of its mechanisms directly linked to the poor:

> They sell the righteous for silver
> > and the needy *('ebyon)* for a pair of sandals [2:6cd, NIV].
> They *trample* [*shwf,* cj] on the heads of the poor *(dal)*
> > as upon the dust of the ground
> and deny *(nth)* justice to the poor *('anaw)* [2:7ab; NIV, "oppressed"].
> You trample *(bshs)* on the poor *(dal)*
> > and force him to give you grain [5:11ab, NIV].
> You deprive *(nth)* the poor *('ebyon)* of justice in the courts [5:12d, NIV].
> You who trample *(sh'f)* the needy *('ebyon)*
> > and do away with *(shbt,* "make to cease") the poor *('anaw)* of the land [8:4ab, NIV].
> buying the poor *(dal)* with silver
> > and the needy *('ebyon)* for a pair of sandals [8:6ab, NIV; cf. 2:6cd, above].

In all, Amos uses explicit vocabulary for oppression only four times (4:1c and 5:12c, cited above, plus *'ashuqim,* in 3:9e). But seven other times his vocabulary for the poor is directly linked to descriptions of *mechanisms* and *metaphorical* language for oppression. A study of metaphorical language for oppression thus might well double the number of Old Testament texts linking oppression to poverty (Elsa Tamez's study points out many of the mechanisms of oppression).

9) *Tsa'aq/za'aq,* "cry out": KB², pp. 810; Hol., pp. 308. Miranda,

following Gunkel and Sarna, argues that this is "a technical term for the cry due to injustice inflicted . . . the anguished cry of the oppressed."[9] Many texts clearly support this conclusion: Exod. 3:7–9; 22:21–23; Ps. 9:13; 107:6. This is not to deny that in certain contexts the meaning may be broader and more general, but the root is especially common in contexts with our basic roots for oppression. Compare the nouns *tse'aqah* and *ze'aqah;* KB[2], p. 263; Hol., p. 91.

10) *Yshb,* "sit, dwell, be enthroned" (some 1,090 times). We should call attention to the conclusions of Norman K. Gottwald regarding the participial form of the root *yshb.* Following previous studies of Albrecht Alt, F. M. Cross, and D. N. Freedman, Gottwald describes the situation in the period Exodus-Judges as follows:

> The *yoshev* (sing.) or *yoshevim* (pl.) are very largely the object of Israel's opposition and attack insofar as they are non-Israelite rulers, or they are the object of severe criticism and threatened punishment insofar as they are Israelite rulers. The term, therefore, has the unmistakable coloration of "ruling abusively" or *"ruling oppressively, "* and at times even the sense of "ruling illegitimately." I can find only a few instances of what appear to be neutral uses of the term in the sense of lacking a negative value judgment [italics added].[10]

Modern translations certainly support the contention that the particle *yoshev* often refers to rulers and not just "inhabitants." Thus in Amos 1:5, 8, NIV translates "the king" with a note "or *the inhabitants of.*" The parallel expression, "the one who holds the sceptor," clearly supports the translation "king."

Of course, Gottwald's epochal study raises the whole question of the proper understanding of the Exodus-Judges period and whether Moses and Joshua were commanded to kill only the corrupt oppressive oligarchy in Canaan ("rulers/kings," not "inhabitants"). This approach may raise as many problems as it solves, but has at least as much to say for it as does traditional conservative apologetics in defending the slaughter of all the *inhabitants* of the land.[11]

IDOLATRY AND NUMEROUS OTHER CAUSES OF POVERTY

My study on oppression and poverty has led me to the conclusion that oppression is perceived in the Old Testament as *the basic cause* of poverty. Frequent lecturing and writing on the subject have shown me that this conclusion is commonly twisted in one of two ways.

Conservative readers easily misread the data to confirm cherished opinions that oppression is one of many in a long list of causes of poverty: "the basic cause" becomes "one of many basic causes," and their theology, ideology, and politics sail through the storm of contradictory data unscathed, so they can affirm with relief when the storm clouds break "there is nothing new under the sun" (Eccles. 1:9; least of all in the Bible! One wonders whatever happened to the old prayer that God would cause fresh light to break forth from his word!).

Marxist-oriented readers easily leap to the conclusion that according to the Bible oppression is the *only* cause of poverty and thus gather ammunition for their revolution to transform oppressive structures, before which all lesser efforts are airily dismissed as "bandaging measles."

Unquestionably the Bible points to a great many possible causes of poverty. To avoid simplistic and inappropriate solutions, we must study carefully the complexity and multiplicity of the causes, without, however, losing sight of what is dominant (oppression). A partial list of causes of poverty indicated in the Bible might be organized as follows:

1) The fall. The fall establishes a relationship of alienation between the human being and God, one's neighbor, and creation, and within the human being. Understood as a space-time event, its chronological priority makes it basic in some ultimate sense. However, it receives little or no mention again in biblical theology until Paul's treatment (Rom. 5:12–21). We find no pairing of the fall with vocabulary for poverty.

2) The alienation now existing between the human person and the creation (ecological causes):
   a. Famine: Gen. 12:10 (Abraham); 26:1 (Isaac); 45:11 (Joseph).
   b. Drought: 1 Kings 17:1–16 (Elijah).
   c. Hurricane, tornado: Job 1:18–19 (Honduras, 1974).
   d. Lightning, fire: Job 1:16.
   e. Earthquakes, volcanos: Gen. 19:24–29 (Nicaragua, 1973; Guatemala, 1976).
   f. Illness, plague, premature death, forced emigration: Ruth 1:1–6; 2 Kings 4:1–7.
   g. Insect plagues: Exod. 7–12; locusts in Joel 1.

But what do the Scriptures suggest to counteract such occurrences? Note especially the case of Joseph in Genesis 41–42; 47:20–26. Here we find such elements as immigration; prophetic warning coupled with preparatory steps; personal charity for special cases; and structural political reform, the institution of a kind of state socialism!

3) The alienation between oneself and one's neighbor:
   a. War: Gen. 14:10–11 (Abraham rescues Lot); 2 Kings 6:24–7:20 (the seige of Samaria in the time of Elisha). To counteract, see Isa. 2:1–5 // Mic. 4:1–4 (the peace and prosperity of the Messiah's reign).
   b. Oppression. Interrelationship of causes should be noted. War is a common mechanism of oppression, as in Judges.

    c. Corrupt government, excessive administrative costs, bureaucratic waste, insensible and unnecessary hierarchies. See 1 Sam. 8:4–5, 10–18, "the ways of a king"; Eccles. 5:8; Neh. 5; Mic. 3:1–4, 9–12; Ezek. 22:23–31; 34.

4) Alienation between the human person and God:

    a. Idolatry (which caused the exiles of 722 and 586 B.C.): 2 Kings 14:26; 17; 21:1–18; 24–25; also many texts in Deuteronomy and Judges (see below for details on idolatry).

    b. Breaking of the Sabbath commandment: Isa. 58:13–14; Neh.13:15–18.

    c. Neglect of the temple: Hag. 1:1–11; 2:6–9, 18–19.

    d. Failure to pay tithes, offerings, care for poor: Mal. 3:6–12; Prov. 3:9–10; Isa. 58:13–14; Neh.13:15–18.

5) Self-alienation (see especially the wisdom literature):

    a. Laziness, sloth: Prov. 6:6–11; 10:4; 19:15; 20:13; 24:30–34; 28:19. But be careful about false accusations: Exod. 5:15–17.

    b. Alcoholism (cf. related drugs today): Prov. 23:19–21; 21:17.

    c. Ignorance, extravagance, waste: Prov. 13:18; 21:5; cf. 3:13 ff.

Conservative evangelicals and conservative Roman Catholics have concentrated too exclusively on the ethical perspectives in the wisdom literature, especially Proverbs, to the neglect of the law and the prophets. Billy Graham and Bill Gothard put great emphasis on the teaching of Proverbs and recommend it for daily reading. This canonical preference reflects and confirms their ideological perception on poverty.

What about other causes of poverty today that are not mentioned in the Bible? On the population explosion, for instance, see Exodus 1:7–8, 22. Note how this text illustrates the need for *relectura*—contextual rereading—instead of simplistic application of biblical texts.

Even a superficial survey thus reveals twenty or more causes of poverty mentioned in the Bible in addition to oppression. It should be noted, however, that these often are directly related to oppression (wars by oppressors), and the vocabulary for poverty/poor occurs overwhelmingly in connection with the vocabulary for oppression. Other causes are either mentioned very few times (sloth, mainly in Proverbs) or not linguistically related to poverty.

The only possible alternative to oppression as a candidate for "the basic cause" of poverty in biblical theology is idolatry. However, the case for idolatry instead of oppression would have to be developed theologically, not linguistically, because there is relatively little overlap between vocabulary for poverty and explicit vocabulary for idolatry in the Bible.

Idolatry is repeatedly indicated as the basic cause of the exile, especially in Jeremiah and Ezekiel. Thus the many texts describing oppression and poverty resulting from the exile might be counted as substantiating the argument for idolatry as the basic cause of poverty. The same would be true for the deuteronomic-type texts in Judges, where a fall into idolatry repeatedly precedes oppression and consequent poverty.

The exodus paradigm, however, does not indict the oppressed Israelites for idolatry: the fault lies with the oppressing Egyptians. In this tradition the eighth-century prophets repeatedly denounce the oppression and idolatry of Israel's rulers—not the idolatry of the poor whom they oppress.

Of course, with a broad theological definition of idolatry ("coveteousness is idolatry," Col. 3:5) all sin comes to be viewed as a manifestation of idolatry, and hence the line between oppression and idolatry is blurred. This kind of theological argument linking oppression and idolatry has in fact been extensively developed by Latin American theologians.[12] Pablo Richard concludes that "the majority of the biblical testimonies about idolatry are found in a context of resistance and struggle against oppression." The religion of the oppressor is by definition idolatrous (Marx's "opiate of the people") because Yahweh is decisively revealed in the exodus as the liberator from oppression, working throughout history to establish justice for the poor. Thus understood, the poverty of Israel in Egypt is traced back to the idolatry of the oppressing pharaoh—and Exodus does include numerous references to "the gods of Egypt."

Hence, if we mean by idolatry the idolatry of oppressors (the pharaoh in Exodus; Israel's oligarchy at the time of the eighth-century prophets), and if we define idolatry in a broad theological way ("covetousness," etc.), then idolatry instead of oppression might be viewed as the basic cause of poverty. But this virtually reduces the conclusion to a platitude: poverty usually is caused by (someone's) sin. Biblical socio-economic analysis, however, contradicts the platitudes of the oppressors. The oppressors (not the oppressed poor) receive the brunt of prophetic indictment, and it is their sin (be it designated oppression, idolatry, covetousness, or whatever) that is viewed as the basic cause of poverty. To argue for idolatry instead of oppression as the basic cause of poverty is to move from clear linguistic data in biblical theology to a broader, more theoretical construct of systematic theology. This may have its value if the sharp socio-economic analysis in the biblical texts is not obscured in the process.

An appropriate Christian strategy against poverty must take into account both normative biblical teaching (both the multiplicity and complexity of causes, and the dominance of oppression as the basic cause) as well as factors from science and "general revelation" (conservatives are usually among the first to emphasize demographic explosion, even though this is *never* viewed in the Bible as a cause for poverty). Obviously, the strategy may vary radically according to concrete historical contexts, but we should be highly suspicious of all efforts that pass lightly over the problem of oppression. Even desperately needed aid to earthquake victims in Somoza's Nicaragua was largely siphoned off by wealthy oppressors. Christian and humanitarian naiveté was providentially overruled, however. The dictator's greed and corruption in the hour of his country's tragic need so alienated the middle class that it led to his downfall.

ISAIAH 53, THE OPPRESSED SERVANT

The Song of the Suffering Servant (more accurately the Oppressed Servant) in Isaiah 53 represents the theological high point of the Old Testament. This chapter also links the two testaments and may be considered the nerve center of biblical theology. No theme basic in Isaiah 53 (a passage often quoted in the New Testament and crucial for New Testament theology) can ever be considered peripheral to the thought of Jesus and his disciples. Isaiah 53, of course, is a fertile field for those who stress *vicarious* penal atonement.[13] But in many theologies of the cross that focus on the trinitarian implications and other profound speculations, the emphasis that Isaiah 53 places on the servant's complete identification with the *oppressed* has not received proper attention.[14] To avoid talking legalistic nonsense when we refer to penal substitution, we must be aware of the *context* in which it occurs.[15] Using four different Hebrew roots, Isaiah 53 refers six times to different dimensions of oppression endured by the servant:

Surely he has borne our griefs
and carried our sorrow;
yet we esteemed him stricken,
smitten by God, and oppressed (*'anah*, pual).
But he was wounded for our transgressions,
he was crushingly oppressed *(daka')* for our iniquities;
upon him was the chastisement that made us whole,
and with his stripes we are healed.

All we like sheep have gone astray;
we have turned every one to his own way;
and the Lord has laid on him
the iniquity of us all.
He was physically oppressed *(nagas)* and he was psychologically
  oppressed (*'anah*, nifal),
yet he opened not his mouth;
like a lamb that is led to the slaughter,
and like a sheep that before its shearers is dumb,
so he opened not his mouth.

By oppression *('otser)* and judgment he was taken away;
and as for his generation, who considered
that he was cut off out of the land of the living,
stricken for the transgression of my people. . . .

Yet it was the will of the Lord to crushingly oppress *(daka')* him
[vv. 4–8, 10].

The prophet stresses all the different kinds of oppression suffered by the Servant: psychological humiliation (*'anah*, vv. 4, 7); physical torture *(daka')*; animal-like degradation (*nagas*, v.7); and judicial injustice (*'oster*, v. 8). In the central section of Isaiah 53 (vv. 4–10) oppression stands out as the main theme, but neither theologians nor biblical commentators have paid any attention to this.

The New Testament focuses on the good news of Jesus Christ for the poor with its center in the cross.[16] Isaiah 53 reminds us that the Suffering Servant is an oppressed servant, whose solidarity with the poor and oppressed is complete. How, then, can we proclaim a biblical gospel without recognizing oppression as a fundamental factor of human life? The church speaks of Jesus as someone who saves us from sin. What the church has not faithfully proclaimed is that according to the Bible sin is not merely an individualistic concept but is also expressed in the structures of oppression. Isaiah reminds us that salvation from sin embraces liberation from oppression (chap. 58; cf. Luke 4:18), because the servant is identified with the poor and oppressed (53:4–10). And these are the texts that Jesus used as the keys to interpret his life, death, and work to his disciples.[17]

CONCLUSIONS

My study of the Hebrew vocabulary for oppression leads me to the following conclusions.

Oppression is a fundamental structural category of biblical theology, as is evidenced by the large number of Hebrew roots denoting it (10 basic roots; 20 in all); the frequency of their occurrence (555 times); the basic theological character of many texts that speak of it (Gen. 15; Exod. 1–5; Ps.72, 103, 146; Isa. 8–9, 42, 53, 58, etc.); and the significance of oppression in Israel's great creedal confession (Deut. 26:5–9).

The virtual absence of this theme in classic theologies, both Catholic (Augustine and Aquinas) and Protestant (Luther, Calvin, Barth, Berkouwer), *stands in astounding contrast to the importance of oppression in biblical theology*. Whether orthodox or liberal, such theologies are found wanting, if not heretical, in dealing with his topic.[18]

Biblical thought is not often explicitly analytical or reflective regarding causality. Nevertheless, careful examination of the texts provides abundant evidence for the conclusion that in biblical theology *oppression is viewed as the basic cause of poverty* (see the 164 texts italicized in the endnotes to chap. 1 and 2, below). In the case of the other 15 to 20 causes for poverty indicated in the Old Testament, the linguistic link is much less frequent—not more than 20 times (e.g., idolatry in Judges; sloth in Proverbs).

The study of the Hebrew vocabulary for oppression shows that *our English translations often hide the radicality of the biblical perception and socio-economic analysis*. Many times they choose mild or ambiguous terms instead of rendering the Hebrew words with their full strength and proper contextual nuance.

In Latin American liberation theologies and in Marxist economic analysis, the theme of oppression plays a commanding role. However, neither Marxist thinkers nor liberation theologians seem aware of the biblical precedents of their analysis that views oppression as the basic cause of poverty.

Neither traditional nor liberation theologians have taken into account the fundamental importance of oppression for properly interpreting the Servant of Isaiah 53, whom we see fulfilled in the New Testament in Jesus Christ (four different terms for oppression appear six times in that chapter).

Finally, to recognize oppression as the basic cause of poverty implies the need of a corresponding Christian response that takes into account the fundamental role of liberation and radical socio-structural changes comparable to the exodus and Jubilee year. Whatever their deficiencies, Latin American liberation theologies contain numerous essential guidelines for biblically faithful proclamation of the gospel of Jesus Christ and for authentic discipleship in a world so characterized by oppression, poverty, and revolution.[19]

SUMMARY CHART

Vocabulary for Oppression
in Relation to Poverty in the Old Testament

I. Basic Hebrew Roots	Total Occurrences, O.T.	Occurrences with Poverty in Context
1. *'shq*	59	31
2. *ynh*	20	15
3. *ngs*	23	20
4. *lḥts*	31	17
5. *rtsts*	20	9
6. *dk'*	31	10
7. *'nh*	82	14
8. ^{II}*tsrr*	96	9
9. ^I*tsrr*	132	10
10. *tsuq*	31	14
II. 10 Less Frequent Hebrew Roots	30	15
Total: 20 Hebrew Roots (lexically defined as "oppress, oppression," etc.)	555	164

Note: The broader meanings of certain roots *('nh,* "oppress, rape, fast," etc.; ^I*tsrr* and ^{II}*tsrr)* result in high occurrences and relatively fewer links to poverty. On the other hand, two words listed under "oppression" *('ani* and ^I*tsarah)* often in themselves mean "poverty" as well as "oppression."

PART TWO

OPPRESSION IN
THE NEW TESTAMENT

Chapter 3

Continuity and Discontinuity

PRESUPPOSITIONS AND METHODOLOGY

My treatment of oppression and poverty begins with a presupposition well expressed by Juan Luis Segundo:

> Christianity is a *biblical* religion. It is the religion of a *book*, of various books if you will, for that is precisely what the word "bible" means. This means that theology for its part cannot swerve from its path in this respect. It must keep going back to its book and reinterpreting it. Theology is not an interpretation of mankind and society, not in the first place at least. [1]

I respect the research and work of specialists in the social sciences who take another point of departure. Rafael Avila suggests the possibility of a dialectic between the two approaches when he writes:

> We are interested in trying to read the Bible *from Latin America*, or perhaps in trying also to read and understand our situation *from the Bible.* [2]

I believe that a fruitful dialectic between the two approaches can result when sociologists and biblical scholars mutually respect each other as priestly members of the same body in which everyone has the privilege and duty to interpret the scriptures, because that function is not the monopoly of the ordained clergy (Jer. 31:31–34; 1 John 2:22–27).

The idea of studying oppression in biblical theology came mainly from a study of liberation theologies. I am particularly grateful to Hugo Assmann for having expounded so well the importance of oppression as a sociological and theological category. [3] Sociology ought not "impose its agenda" (much less its conclusions) on biblical theology, but biblical theology today, I believe, must take many of the questions and concerns of the social sciences seriously—

especially when such topics deeply penetrate the church's theological reflection. To ignore such concerns could result in losing the prophetic message ("what the Spirit is telling the churches" [including members who are social scientists]) and in denying the church's identity as the body of Christ.

Therefore the norm that we work from is the Bible, true (or inerrant, as many prefer) in all that it teaches. Furthermore I am convinced that we are living in an age when God through his grace is causing much new light to burst from his word. My concern is to call attention to the positive dimensions of a biblical message that until now has smoldered in darkness. Other Evangelicals are concentrating their efforts on pointing out the risks and extremes involved in this new challenge, but have said very little that has not been said first and often better by liberation theologians themselves. More than anything else, I wish to search out the path illuminated by the light of the Bible.

Some will surely criticize my methodology by calling it a kind of "biblical positivism" in the tradition (and with the presuppositions) of B. B. Warfield.[4] No harm done. I do not claim that mine is the only valid methodology, or the only one that leads to truth.[5] The Spirit blows where it wills and can communicate the truth by means of (or despite) whatever methodology used in any serious attempt to approach God in his word.

In the first part of this study the methodology used was simple enough: I looked for the word "oppression" in Young's *Analytical Concordance,* noting the Hebrew and Greek words so translated. After that I consulted the Hebrew and Greek lexicons, along with concordances based on those languages. I studied every example of the words in the semantic area related to oppression. By studying both the lexicons and the texts where that basic vocabulary of oppression occurs, I discovered several additional words and texts. Considering the rich variety of Hebrew words in this semantic area, I tried to define the special nuances of each word, and I drew exegetical and theological conclusions from that work. For this English edition of my study my son Stanley read through Holladay's lexicon and uncovered several additional Hebrew roots that had eluded previous pursuit. All this may sound shockingly elementary, but as C. S. Lewis warns us, biblical scholars (conservative inerrantists as well as liberal higher critics) sometimes gaze so long at "fern seed" that they fail to see the elephants.

When I turned to the New Testament, a word-based focus at first glance yielded few results. Few texts use words such as "oppression" explicitly, and all are found in James and Luke-Acts. I was faced with the problem of an apparent lack of continuity between the Old and New Testaments. Therefore I chose to study James and Luke-Acts according to the *ideas* expressed in order to trace how the *theme* of oppression developed in the New Testament. Talks with several experts in the field (especially Plutarco Bonilla and Richard Foulkes) and reading several works suggested by Orlando Costas (especially that of Juan Luis Segundo) put me on new trails for development of the theme. More than anything else, reading Luke-Acts in Greek several times suggested new perspectives, because the word studies had produced some awareness of the theme and of the dimensions obscured in the standard translations.

Studying the vocabulary of persecution, I stumbled on what amounts to the obscuring of such words as *thlīpsis* and *thlíbo* when the standard translations render them with such weak terms as "affliction" and "tribulation."

The entire process well illustrates the third step in the "hermeneutic circle" that Juan Luis Segundo speaks of as:

> . . . a new way of experiencing theological reality that leads us to exegetical suspicion, that is, to the suspicion that the prevailing interpretation of the Bible has not taken important pieces of data into account.[6]

I hope that other scholars better trained in Greek and in New Testament studies will be able to complement this elementary effort with more satisfactory results (see chap. 1, note 29). In addition, further study of the Old Testament according to the development of the *concept* of oppression could open up new horizons of scholarship for us.

Finally, I should like to highlight my position on the role played by presuppositions, both theological and ideological. Obviously presuppositions inevitably *influence* one's work—perhaps more than anything else in selecting an area for investigation. However, they should never *determine* one's conclusions. The history of theology abounds with examples of scholars who started with presuppositions of one sort and changed them for another kind in the course of their work (popular examples are the works of Frank Morris on the resurrection and William Ramsey on the historicity of Luke-Acts). If one is aware of one's presuppositions, they will remain out in the open where lightning bolts from new data may destroy them, or at least radically modify them.

CONTINUITY: JAMES—PROPHETIC FURY

In the biblical theology of oppression we may say that the Letter of James shows *continuity* between the New and the Old Testaments.

The author of this letter may indeed be the brother of Jesus (as many New Testament experts continue to believe). Especially if that be the case, we should think twice before relegating oppression to "another dispensation" (pre-Christian; materialistic and political) that does not approach the spiritual heights of Jesus and Paul.[7]

James recognizes class struggle as an inevitable dimension of reality (a truth Marx *re*discovered and stressed but did not create):

> Is it not the rich who oppress *(katadunasteuō)* you, is it not they who drag you into court? [James 2:6b].

James emphasizes that the churches he addresses identify with the lot of the poor, and in fact count most of their members from the poor:

> Has not God chosen those who are poor in the world to be rich in faith and heirs of the kingdom which he has promised to those who love him? [v. 2:5; cf. 1:9].

Why is it that in all our enormous tomes about predestination (especially in the Augustinian and Calvinist tradition) one always goes away with the impression that God elected the middle class and not the poor? In studying the "inscrutable decrees," we should at least clearly affirm what the word of God makes obvious, as Deuteronomy 29:29 insists.

James places himself firmly in the ranks of the prophets who viewed oppression as the *basic reason* for poverty (2:1-7; 5:1-6). Never does he shift the blame to the poor themselves, because of racial inferiority, laziness, vices, or other reasons. The rich bear the basic guilt, because they exploit and oppress:

> Look: the wages you failed to pay the workmen who mowed your fields are crying out against you. The cries of the harvesters have reached the ears of the Lord all-powerful [5:5].

The church, the brotherhood of the poor, is viewed as God's initial response to the problem of poverty. It is a scandal if the church does not anticipate the culmination of the kindgom by caring for the needs of its neediest members:

> If a brother or sister is ill clad and in lack of daily food, and one of you says to him, "Go in peace, be warmed and filled," without giving them the things needed for the body, what does it profit? [2:15-16].

Furthermore it is not merely the genuineness of individual faith, but the church's very authenticity that is at stake in this activity. It befits the church to respond to requests, but more importantly, to take the initiative in *searching out* needy persons. God judges the church, not for its orthodoxy, but for its orthopraxy:

> Religion that is pure and undefiled before God and the Father is this: to visit orphans and widows in their oppression *(thlīpsis)*[8] and to keep oneself unstained from the world [1:27].

We should recall that in the Old Testament the orphans and widows (along with foreigners or immigrants) became the prototypes of the oppressed classes. Similarly, the church's authenticity depends on its commitment to the oppressed.

God's final response in the face of oppression and its resulting poverty is the Lord's return:

Therefore [cf. the previous context, 5:1-6] be patient, brethren, until the coming *(parousía)* of the Lord *(kurios;* cf. 1:1). . . . behold the judge is standing at the doors [5:7, 9].

We can compare this to Acts 1:8, where Luke does not reject political liberation as a dimension of Christian salvation but rather links it above all to the second coming for its full realization.

In addition (and here James transcends the Old Testament perspective and anticipates Luke's theology), such liberation as characterizes the church is evident especially in healing miracles (cf. the plagues in Exodus) and in forgiveness of sins.

Is anyone among you suffering? Let him pray. Is any cheerful? Let him sing praise. Is any among you sick? Let him call for the elders of the church, and let them pray over him, anointing him with oil in the name of the Lord; and the prayer of faith will save *(sódzo)* the sick, and the Lord will raise him up; and if he has committed sins, he will be forgiven *(aphíemi;* cf.Luke 4:18) [James 5:13-15].

In such texts as these we can see that "salvation" in biblical theology includes physical health as a foreshadowing of full political liberation.Thus Evangelical theologians are mistaken if they deny that physical healing and political liberation are dimensions of the salvation that Christ brings us. Biblical theology teaches us to think more synthetically and not create so many dichotomies, as is the custom in traditional theologies dominated by Greek philosophy.[9]

THLĪPSIS: THE LEXICONS AND THE TRANSLATIONS

As I have already indicated in studying James 1:27, "oppression" is to be preferred as the translation of the noun *thlīpsis*.[10] The most authoritative Greek lexicons give "oppression" as the first meaning. However, our common translations never translate *thlīpsis* by "oppression"! On the contrary they are content to use softer, more ambiguous terms such as "affliction," "tribulation," "difficulty," "suffering," and the like.[11] I do not say that these are mistaken translations, but I insist that in many instances in the New Testament *thlīpsis* expresses definite socio-economic nuances that common translations suppress or veil. This is also true regarding the verb *thlíbo.* I have mentioned that James refers to the *thlīpsis* suffered by widows and orphans, classes commonly oppressed in the Old Testament. Both the immediate and general contexts in James reveal the oppression commonly suffered by the church as a brotherhood of poor workers (2:6; 5:4).

But if this is the case among the Christians in James, why should we think that the situation is different elsewhere? In Acts we read about the economic impact that the gospel caused in Ephesus because the sales of idols had plummeted (19:23–27). Revelation 13 tells of a boycott as a reprisal against the Christians who do not worship "the beast."

Thus when Christ addresses the church in Smyrna he says, "I know your oppression ("tribulation," RSV, NAB; "trials," JB; "that you are hard pressed," NEB; Greek: *thlīpsis*) and your poverty" (Rev. 2:9; cf. v. 10). Both the overall context of the book and the link with poverty support the translation "oppression" instead of "affliction." In an important article on the theology of the Book of Revelation, Juan Stam has pointed to the fierceness with which Revelation criticizes (especially in chaps. 18 and 19) the economic oppression by the Roman empire.[12] But if this is the case in Revelation 2, 13, 18, and 19, why need we think that the "great tribulation" *(thlīpsis)* in 7:14 does not also include the element of oppression?[13]

In the letter to the Hebrews we read:

> But recall the former days when, after you were enlightened, you endured a hard struggle with sufferings, sometimes being publicly exposed to abuse and oppression *(thlīpsis)* and sometimes being partners with those so treated. For you had compassion on the prisoners, and you joyfully accepted the plundering of your property, since you knew that you yourselves had a better possession and an abiding one [10:32–34].

Several factors suggest that in this context we should understand *thlīpsis* to mean not just "affliction" in a general sense, but something like the oppression suffered by the disciples in James's letter. Hebrews was probably written (by Barnabas?) around A.D. 65 to some Jewish converts in Palestine, perhaps to a group of priests who had originally converted to Christianity in Jerusalem (Acts 6:7).[14] The public baptism ("after you became enlightened," 10:32) of such persons would have provoked systematic and oppressive economic measures. The well-to-do converted priests thus became "partners" (*koinonoi*, 10:33) in solidarity with ordinary believers and the poor. They lost their inheritances along with other goods and property in the face of oppressive plundering (undoubtedly under a pretext of legality). But they happily accepted this instead of tangling themselves in useless legal battles in the corrupt courts dominated by their rivals (1 Cor. 6:1–8).[15] Hebrews points ahead to the Messiah's imminent return, just as does James, and to the just final judgment (10:37). Thus these converted priests find themselves in the same tradition with the devout poor and oppressed of the Old Testament, those who lived without clothing and shelter, "the poor, oppressed *(thlībo)*, and mistreated" (11:32). As we have seen many times in the Old Testament, the basic cause of poverty here is not inferiority ("of whom the world was not worthy," 11:38), but oppression. Thus it seems that Hebrews 10:32–34 is not speaking of occasional robbery, but rather of the continuing "class struggle" so characteristic of the Old Testament and of James. Oppression served as the tool of Palestine's dominating class, the rich and unconverted oligarchy.

Paul too shows that often we must understand *thlīpsis* and *thlībo* in terms of oppression. Both words occur frequently in 2 Corinthians where the context explicitly relates oppression and poverty. When Paul describes the reaction of the churches in Macedonia, he writes:

> for in a severe test of *oppression* [*thlīpsis*], their abundance of joy and their extreme *poverty* have overflowed in a wealth of liberality on their part [8:2, cf. 6:4, 10; 12:10].

Here we find the same elements (oppression, poverty, joy) as in Hebrews and James. Poverty is not seen as a result of some sin or racial inferiority, but of oppression. And, as in the case of the widow in Luke 21:1-4, generosity appears as a characteristic of the poor and not of the rich—who have become rich because of greed and oppression.When 1 Corinthians 7:26 refers to "necessity" *('anánke)*, it could well be referring to the same kind of oppression that we have seen in James and Hebrews.

Paul uses *thlīpsis* and *thlíbo* often in the Letters to the Thessalonians (1 Thess.1:6; 3:3; 7; 2 Thess. 1:4, 6). *Thlīpsis* and *thlíbo* accompany the rejection of idolatry (1 Thess. 1:6; cf. Acts 19) and persecution (1 Thess. 1:4). J. B. Lightfoot highlights the church's poverty when he writes:

> They were baptized with the baptism of suffering, and this suffering was the result both of poverty and of persecution. There is no warning against the temptations of wealth, no enforcement of the duties of the rich, in the Epistles to the Thessalonians or Philippians. The former especially are addressed as those who have to work for their living.[16]

We find further evidence for relating oppression, poverty, and persecution in Romans:

> Who shall separate us from the love of Christ? Shall oppression (*thlīpsis*), or distress, or persecution, or famine, or nakedness, or peril, or sword? As it is written, "For thy sake we are being killed all the day long; we are regarded as sheep to be slaughtered" [8:35-36].

As H. Schlier says, "the series in Romans 8:35 lists seven kinds of *thlīpsis*"[17]—that is, seven kinds of *oppression*! Persecution in this case is one kind of oppression, especially if the authorities cooperated with zealous religious leaders and thus misused the power of the sword. When Paul deals with the persecution of the church, he quotes Psalm 44:14, in which the original context speaks explicitly of the *oppression* of Israel (*dacah*, v. 20; *'ani* and *lahats*, v. 25).[18] Obviously, therefore, we should translate *thlīpsis* "oppression" and not "tribulation." *Thlīpsis* is something the poor church suffered, something that in the context is related to references of hunger and nakedness. The elements in the immediate context point to the continuity of Pauline thought with the situation of the Old Testament psalm.

If this is the case in Paul's letters where we have such explicit clues, it may well be that in many other texts we should understand *thlīpsis* and *thlībo* as referring to oppression and to the class struggle along the lines of the exodus experience, and not simply as affliction in some vague sense.

What do we say, therefore, of Jesus himself? The parable of the sower contrasts those who suffer oppression *(thlīpsis)* and persecution *(diogmós)*, which arises because of the word (Mark 4:17, Matt. 13:21), with those whose temptations are different because they lead different lives—"the delight in riches and the desire for other things" (Mark 4:16–17; 18–19). Thus, just as in the case of James, Hebrews, and Paul, we notice an implicit contrast between the oppressed poor and their rich oppressors. If this is the case, should we not understand that the references to the "great tribulation" (Mark 13:19, 24; Matt. 24:9, 21, 29) include elements of economic oppression, just as is the case in the great tribulation of Revelation 13:6, 7, 18, 19?

Thus I conclude that many times the best choice for translating *thlīpsis* and *thlībo* would be "oppression" and "oppress." I base this conclusion on the continuity of Old Testament perspectives, on Jesus' mission to the oppressed (Luke 4:18, 19), and on the express situation of the Christians in James and Acts 10:38 and various other New Testament texts that connect oppression with poverty and its results. If we so translate, obviously the theme of oppression is much more common in the New Testament than our common Bible translations lead us to understand. We can even say that the New Testament is stronger in a certain sense than the Old Testament because "the constant tribulation *(thlīpsis)* of Israel in the Old Testament has become the Church's *necessary* tribulation in the New Testament."[19] And, as in the Old Testament, the link between poverty and oppression shows that oppression continues also in the New Testament to be the basic cause of poverty.[20]

DISCONTINUITY: LUKE-ACTS— CHARISMATICS FOR REVOLUTION

In approaching this theme, I ought to warn that neither the political context in which Luke moved nor his purposes in writing Luke-Acts lent themselves to an explicit, detailed treatment of oppression, something that the Roman rulers easily could have misunderstood. We may compare, for example, the title "messiah" cautiously used in the gospels, and the wrath of God (repugnant to the Greek mind) and hence much more common in the Old Testament. Prudent writers carefully choose their words after considering who their readers are and what are their main purposes in writing.[21]

To understand Luke's writings in relation to the theology of oppression, poverty, and liberation, we must first recall Jesus' and the church's political context.

Christian apologists have praised Luke for carefully using the correct titles in referring to Roman officials. F. F. Bruce insists (correctly, I think) that this demonstrates Luke's capacity as a trustworthy historian.[22] At times we forget that this is also proof of Luke's subtle sensitivity to political affairs. James, in relative security (Jerusalem), could denounce oppression with a kind of prophetic fury. Luke, on the other hand, in the delicate situation of the heathen world (perhaps even with Paul's life in the balance) was walking on eggs.

In the prophetic songs at the beginning of his Gospel, Luke shows that God's people still spoke with the same awareness of being an oppressed people as it had done in Old Testament times (Luke 1:51-55, 68-79). It is still a poor, humble, and oppressed people, longing for political liberation. The disciples' question at the beginning of Acts (1:6, 7) reflects the same viewpoint. But Luke addresses himself to Theophilus, not to harden his heart with vengeful plagues (Exodus), but with the hope that Theophilus be confirmed in acceptance of the gospel truth. Not for a moment, however, does Luke obscure the gospel's message concerning the poor and oppressed.

Commentators have pointed out a series of texts in Luke-Acts, showing that the author sought to win the same freedom for the church to proclaim the gospel that the Jews already enjoyed in practicing their religion.[23] Furthermore we must emphasize that the Romans were not the ones primarily guilty of oppressing God's people; the Jewish politico-religious oligarchy was the primary oppressor. As Juan Luis Segundo points out:

> If we agree with Gutiérrez that the realm of politics is the most prevalent and pervasive factor in present-day human life, it is anachronistic to ask what Jesus' attitude might have been towards this *present-day* situation of ours. The discovery of the pervasive influence of politics is our contemporary discovery, not his. Hence Jesus' stance vis-à-vis the Roman Empire or the Zealots, as a political stance, is also relatively beside the point. The fact is that the concrete, systematic oppression that Jesus confronted in his day did not appear to him as "political" in our sense of the term; it showed up to him as "religious" oppression. More than officials of the Roman Empire, it was the religious authority of the Scribes and Sadducees and Pharisees that determined the socio-political structure of Israel. In real life this authority was political, and Jesus really did tear it apart. This is evident from the fact that the concern to get rid of Jesus physically—because he threatened the status quo—was primarily displayed by the supposedly "religious" authorities rather than by the representatives of the Roman Empire.[24]

Later he adds:

> . . . we are guilty of an anachronism when we assume that the decisive and critical political plane—precisely in political terms—was the opposition between Judea and the Roman Empire. It is quite possible that some contemporary groups such as the Zealots thought it was. But it seems to me that the political reality that really structured the Israel of Jesus' time and determined people's role and relationships in society was not the Roman Empire but the Jewish theocracy grounded on, and

controlled by, the religious authorities who had charge of the Mosaic Law. We have already noted how Jesus destroyed the foundation of that oppressive power structure by teaching the people to reject its theological foundations. His teaching was such a political threat that the authorities of Israel made use of Rome's authorities to eliminate this dangerous *political* adversary. That is precisely what Jesus was.[25]

Segundo's clarifications are extremely valuable. In Evangelical circles, especially those rooted in the Anabaptist tradition, the rigid doctrine of separation of church and state unduly influences hermeneutics. (I shall not here debate the value of this distinction as a strategy and political principle for church praxis.) We tend to think of the Roman empire as "the state" and the Jewish authorities as "the church." We forget that in a theocracy, as Judaism was during the first century, such a distinction simply does not exist (not to mention the Roman empire's emphatically religious element, unmasked in Revelation).

If Segundo's analysis of Israel's political situation and of Jesus' political tactics is correct, the implications for our study of oppression in the New Testament are obvious. The question remains whether Christians in Latin America should not also concentrate more on the tyrannical local oligarchies that encourage such great foreign exploitation, instead of consuming so much energy denouncing foreign imperialism—a force that goes its merry way, deaf to all such cries. Perhaps we prefer a long life, comfortable but useless, to martyrdom!

Luke 4:18–19 and the Theology of Oppression

The interpretation of Luke 4:18–19 makes clear two additional factors that help us understand the theology of oppression in the New Testament. In this text Jesus defines his gospel as an announcement of the good news to the *poor* and *oppressed*.[26] As Herman Ridderbos points out:

> These "poor" or "poor in spirit" (meek) . . . represent the socially oppressed, those who suffer from the power of injustice and are harassed by those who only consider their own advantage and influence. They are, however, at the same time those who remain faithful to God and expect their salvation from his kingdom alone.[27]

Ridderbos understands the "poor" of Luke 4:18 in the light of Matthew's fourth beatitude, which was spoken to those "who hunger and thirst for justice." Ridderbos compares this text with the parable of the unjust judge (Luke 18:1–8) and concludes that the "justice mentioned here is nothing but the deliverance (from oppression) to which God's people (his elect) may lay claim as the salvation promised them by their King."[28]

The ''poor'' continues to be an important category in New Testament theology (*ptōchós,* for example, occurs 34 times in the New Testament, 10 times in Luke).[29] The vocabulary denoting oppression is less explicit, but in Luke 4:18 we clearly see the continuity with the Old Testament perspective: the poor are the oppressed; that is why they are poor.

Another important element is that, in the context of Luke 4:18, Jesus points to his ministry as the time of fulfillment (4:21) and of announcing the good news to the poor. We have seen how the Old Testament keenly analyzed and unmasked the causes of poverty, showing the primary one to be oppression. Now, with Jesus' proclamation, the time for poking around in a rubble heap of *causes* has come to an end: it is time to proclaim the arrival of the *solution*—the kingdom of God! In Acts we will see how Luke delineates this solution.

Acts 10:38 and the Theology of Oppression

Segundo calls attention to a basic factor that we must take into account when he writes:

> Jesus himself seems to focus his message on liberation at the level of interpersonal relationships, forgetting almost completely, if not actually ruling out, liberation vis-à-vis political oppression. The same would seem to apply to Paul and almost all the other writings in the New Testament.[30]

Segundo partly explains the situation with his broad definition of politics and by his analysis of the political situation in which Jesus and the church lived. Nevertheless, Acts 10:38 offers us additional perspectives by emphasizing the radical change that the theme of oppression undergoes in the New Testament. In this text, Peter, preaching in the house of Cornelius, summarizes Jesus' entire ministry by saying:

> [You know] how God anointed Jesus of Nazareth with the Holy Spirit and with power, how he went about doing good and healing all that were oppressed *(katadunasteúō)* by the devil, for God was with him [10:38].

Suddenly a new element in the New Testament theology of oppression leaps into view. What Jesus does for the oppressed does not appear to be a socio-political liberation, such as that of Moses: instead he is *healing.* That is, according to Peter's interpretation we ought to understand all the healings that Jesus and his disciples performed in Luke-Acts as *liberation of oppressed persons.* These healings take the place of the plagues of the exodus. And as the plagues did, they bring God's people into a series of confrontations with the ecclesio-political authorities. They witness to the gospel, instead of merely proclaiming vindictive judgments. Nevertheless, freedom from sickness should not be misinterpreted in biblical theology as something purely individualistic and of less political consequence than the exodus. On the contrary, such a liberation represents an attack against death itself, the mighty tyrant and "last enemy" (1 Cor.15:26). Thus in comparison with the exodus this is a great leap forward in the process of human liberation, not a depoliticized step backward.

Furthermore Peter points to the devil himself as the agent behind all oppression, the one who takes the place of the pharaoh of the exodus. Again the text presents a revolutionary perspective. This partly explains why Paul insisted that the conflict waged by the people of God is not against flesh and blood, but against the principalities and powers behind all human government.[31] The new perspective does not replace a political perspective with a different "spiritual" perspective, but instead it shows us the diabolical dimension behind the political one (a factor not yet explicit in Exodus).

Perhaps the Lukan text that most emphasizes that healings are liberation from diabolical oppression is Luke 13:10–17, where Jesus cures a hunch-backed old woman. Luke introduces the story by saying that the woman "had a spirit of infirmity" (v. 11), and when Jesus freed her, he called her a "daughter of Abraham whom Satan [had] bound for eighteen years" (v. 16).

In the parable of the unjust judge and the importunate widow (an oppressed class) Luke again underlines the reality of oppression-poverty-liberation so dominant in his theology, though he carefully avoids highly provocative terms (18:1–8). The widow comes demanding justice from her adversary (*'antidíkou*, "oppressor"). This parable makes it impossible to think of preaching the good news of the kindgom without including the dimension of political liberation:

> Hear what the unrighteous judge says. And will not God vindicate his elect [poor-oppressed] who cry to him day and night? Will he delay long over them? [v. 6, 7].

These words resemble the prophetic tone of James (2:5; 5:1–6), but by the indirect means of a parable.

Acts 1–12: Liberation and Justice

When we study the *structure* of Acts 1–12 with an eye to the theology of oppression-poverty-liberation (Luke 14:18 and Acts 10:30), certain conclusions impose themselves. Six times in Acts 1–12 the same five basic elements repeat themselves:

1) acts of liberation (miracles, mainly healings);
2) proclamation of the good news to the poor;
3) conflicts with the politico-religious oppressors and testimony before them;
4) justice for the oppressed poor in the new community;
5) expansion of the church (consisting mostly of poor persons).

I offer the following structural analysis (which does not pretend to be an exact outline of the book) simply to highlight key elements:

First Cycle: 2:1–47
1. The miracle of Pentecost, 1–13, 19.
2. Proclamation of the good news to the poor, 14–41, especially v.18 (the Spirit given to the poor).
3. Denunciation of oppression, 23, 36, 40.
4. Justice for the poor of the new community, 42, 44–45.
5. Favor with the masses, 47a.

Second Cycle: 3:1–4:37
1. Liberation-healing of a lame man, 3:1–10; cf. the liberation of Peter and John from prison, 3:13–22.
2. Proclamation of the good news to the poor, 3:11–26.
3. Conflict and testimony before authorities, 4:1–31; oppression denounced, 4:10–11, 27.
4. Justice for the poor in the new community, 4:32–37.
5. Growth of the church, 4:31, 33.

Third Cycle: 5:1–6:7
1. Plagues and signs (that the messianic age has come), 5:1–16 (death of Ananias and Saphira [1–11], acts of liberation/healings [12–16]); liberation of apostles from prison, 5:19.
2. Conflict and testimony before authorities, 5:17–42; oppression denounced, 5:28, 30.
3. Proclamation of the good news to the poor, 5:20–21, 25, 42.
4. Deacons guarantee justice for the poor, 6:1–6.
5. Growth of the church, 6:7 (cf. 5:14).

Fourth Cycle: 6:8–9:42
1. Acts of liberation by Stephen, 6:8, Philip, 8:6–8, 13; Peter, 9:32–35, 36–41.
2. Conflict and testimony before authorities, 6:9–8:3; oppression denounced, 6:13–14; 7:6, 9, 19, 23, 51–54; witness before a ruler, 8:26–40; an oppressor-persecutor converted, 9:1–31.
3. Proclamation of the good news to the poor, 7:56; 8:4–5, 12, 25, 40; cf. 8:34–35 (Isa. 56:3–7); 9:42.
4. Dorcas's exemplary ministry to widows (oppressed class), 9:36–41.
5. Growth of the church, 9:42 (cf. 9:31).

Fifth Cycle: 10:1–11:30
1. Miracle of Cornelius's conversion, 10:1–48; 11:1–18.
2. Proclamation of the good news, 10:34–43; 11:19–20.
3. Denunciation of oppression, 10:39.
4. Justice for the poor in the Gentile world, 10:2, 4, 35; extends from Antioch to Jerusalem, 11:27–30.
5. Growth of the church, 11:21–26.

Sixth Cycle: 12:1–16
    1. Oppression of the Jerusalem church, 1–5.
    2. Liberation of Peter from prison, 6–17.
    3. Denunciation and death of Herod, the idolatrous oppressor, 18–23.
    4. Growth of the church, v. 24.
    5. Justice for the poor, v. 25 (in Jerusalem).

We can see, therefore, how in Acts 1–12 Luke emphasizes miraculous liberation of the oppressed-poor and justice for them within the Palestine church. This effective liberating activity stands out as the point of departure for an effective proclamation of the good news to the poor and for the church's growth. The miracles (healing, liberating prisoners, etc.) that accompany the preaching of the gospel propel the church into a constant confrontation with the oppressive politico-religious authorities and result in testimony before them. We should understand these acts of liberation as *signs* of the arrival of the messianic age, in which there is justice for the oppressed-poor.[32] This is how Acts 1–12 looks when viewed from the perspective of the oppressed-poor and Jesus' own "theology of liberation" (Luke 4:18–19).

Acts 13–28: Mission and Oppression-Persecution

In Acts 13–28 Luke no longer focuses his interest on healing miracles, justice for the church's poor, and its growth. Instead of considering the growth of the church in Palestine, now Luke wishes to concentrate on its expansion throughout the Roman empire. The liberations signaling the arrival of the messianic age are not so often of the sick and prisoners, but miracles of a very different sort: the conversion of the gentiles. The "pilot project" of the coming kingdom (the church in Palestine) not only extends but *multiplies* in the entire gentile world (just as Israel had to do before the exodus, Exod. 1:1–7).

In the Old Testament God sought to *separate* his people in one country. Because of this, Moses instigated the exodus in the first place so that the Israelites could "hold a feast in the wilderness" (Exod. 5:1, etc.). In contrast (as Luke reminds us in the conclusion of his work), the church's goal in the New Testament is to proclaim the gospel freely in all the world (Acts 28: 30–31). Nehemiah's wall well symbolizes the separation that God intended for the Old Testament. But the "highway in the desert" (Isa. 40:3) comes to signal how the gospel penetrated the world in the New Testament era, fulfilling the divine purpose (Mark 1:3, Matt. 3:3, Luke 3:4).

In Acts 13–28 Paul, the converted oppressor, occupies center stage. But what Paul had fomented and was now suffering is oppression in the form of persecution.[33] In general we might say that oppression stems from greed, but that persecution arises from religious zeal (John 15:18–25). Because of this, persecution became more common after the people of God set out to preach in the pagan world. The emphasis on persecution reflects the church's new dynamic and more mobile situation. Nevertheless, the New Testament church continued to be poor (1 Cor. 1:26-29), hence also oppressed (James). Persecution, motivated by religious zeal, goes hand in hand with oppression, caused by greed. We should not think that persecution takes the place of oppression. When they set out to preach the good news to the pagan world, the poor people of God became not only the oppressed, but also those persecuted by peoples of other faiths.

Concern for the poor in Acts 13-28 is evident primarily in the divine protection that Paul enjoyed as the poor man *par excellence* (Acts 20:32-35; 26:17; cf. 2 Cor. 6:3-10; 1 Cor. 4:8-13). Also we may recall the offerings the gentile churches gave for the poor in Jerusalem (24:17; cf. 11:27-30; 12:25). Paul and Luke surely understood these offerings as further signs of the arrival of the messianic age (Isa. 60:5-7, 13; 61:6-7; 66:12).[34]

The transition from healing miracles and justice for the poor in Acts 1-12 to the focus on the miracle of gentile conversions in Acts 13-28 helps us understand another factor: oppression in the latter section is not seen primarily as sickness but as diabolical darkness that instigates oppression in the form of persecution. In order to understand something of this development in the theology of oppression-poverty-liberation in Acts 13-28, we must carefully compare Paul's commission in Acts 26 with Jesus' in Luke 4:

Luke 4:18-19	Acts 26:17-18
The Spirit of the Lord is upon me, because he has anointed me to preach good news to the poor. He has *sent* me to proclaim *release* to the captives and recovery of *sight to the blind*, to set at *liberty* those who are *oppressed,* to proclaim the *acceptable year* of the Lord.	Delivering you from the people and from the Gentiles—to whom I *send* you to *open their eyes,* that they may turn from darkness to light and from the *power of Satan* to God, that they may receive *forgiveness* of sins and an *inheritance* among those who are sanctified by faith in me.

In this context we see Paul recounting his story to Agrippa (his oppressor). He tells how he himself quit oppressing and persecuting the church in order to identify himself with the oppressed and the persecuted. First Paul quotes Jesus' promise to liberate him from oppression and persecution. Jesus' physical healing of the blind becomes a *universal spiritual enlightenment* in Paul's commission. The conversion that results from the universal enlightenment becomes in Paul's commission a liberation from Satan the oppressor. But the word "forgiveness" (Greek: *áphesis*) in Paul is the same that is rendered "release" and "liberty" in Luke 4:18. The reference to the Year of Jubilee in Luke 4:19 finds its parallel in the reference to the inheritance (Greek: *klēros*, "inheritance, assigned portion") in Acts 26:18.[35]

Thus when we compare these two commissions we can notice common elements that have developed distinctly. We should not understand the change as a "spiritualization" in the Greek sense (thus deprecating the material); nor does Paul in any way "depoliticize" the gospel. The messianic signs of healing and freeing of prisoners in Luke 4:18–19 nearly always become in Paul the miracle of the conversion of gentiles (Isa. 42:6, 7; 49:6, 7; cf. 35:5–6). But they are surely also *evidence that the kingdom of God has arrived.* In Paul's commission all the oppressive powers—physical sickness, economic injustice, political tyranny—are exposed as expressions of "Satan's authority."[36] Once more it is evident that forgiveness of sins is just *one* dimension of the salvation that Paul preached.[37]

Summary and Synthesis: Luke-Acts

We have seen that Luke, in the same way as James, demonstrates a basic continuity with the Old Testament perspective of oppression: God's people speaks with a profound awareness of being a politically oppressed people (prophetic songs in Luke 1–2; cf. Acts 1:8), and in Luke 4:18–19 "the poor" continue to be synonymous with "the oppressed." Nevertheless what is most notable in Luke-Acts is how the author develops and extends the theme of oppression:

1) The primary oppressor (the one behind the power of the pharaohs and the local oligarchies) is revealed as the *devil* himself (Acts 10:38). Therefore the arms used to combat this power must give priority to prayer and the word (Acts 4:23–31).

2) On the human level, Luke is not so much interested in analyzing the *causes* of poverty (as the Old Testament so often did) as in putting into practice and proclaiming the *solution* in God's kingdom (with the church and its praxis as the "pilot project").

3) In Luke oppression is most evident as illness (Acts 10:38).

4) Jesus gives priority to *healing* the oppressed and not to immediate liberation from Rome's yoke. Nevertheless the miracles (largely healings) surely have political significance, because they result in a confrontation with the politico-religious authorities.

5) Political liberation manifests itself in destroying the Jewish religious hierarchy's oppressive authority (scribes, Pharisees, Sadducees), freeing their prisoners, and in winning religious liberty for openly preaching the gospel throughout the Roman empire (Acts 28:30–31).

6) The oppressed-poor enjoy the benefits of the Year of Jubilee (Luke 4:19; Lev. 25) within the bosom of the church where God's purposes for his coming *universal kingdom* begin to be evident (Acts 1–12).

7) Even as the good news of the kingdom spreads throughout the world, the church continues to suffer oppression, now no longer merely as a static economic class, but also as itinerant persecuted missionaries (especially Paul, Acts 13–28).

Therefore we recognize that in Luke-Acts *sickness, hierarchical religious tyranny, persecution, and imprisonment become the principal forms of oppression.* In the face of all this, Jesus Christ is proclaimed as the liberator: healing the sick, unmasking false claims of authorities, protecting and liberating his witnesses—often miraculously. "Salvation" for Luke is certainly integral liberation, and not without its politico-economic dimension.

CONCLUSIONS

In the 1970s two movements made a great impact on the church in Latin America. On the one hand we saw the charismatic-pentecostal movement with its emphasis on healing miracles and huge campaigns in which a supposedly "depoliticized gospel" is preached. On the other hand liberation theologies (with leftist political orientation) challenged political and religious authorities. These two movements have gone their separate ways almost without contacting one another.

Perhaps the most important lesson we can learn from studying oppression in Luke-Acts is that in the New Testament such a dichotomy between these two dimensions did not exist. The proclamation of the kingdom was accompanied by miraculous healings and exorcisms, but the church's praxis and preaching were such that the healings and sermons led inevitably to a clash with the political authorities and resulted in Christian witness before them. As a result authorities sometimes were converted and showed good will to the church (with varying degrees of political liberation, depending on the power of a given official), or if the officials were not converted persecution intensified. In Acts 28:16 the last report shows Jesus' emissary under guard of a Roman soldier (cf. Paul's predecessor, John the Baptist!). This suggests the relativity of political liberations resulting from gospel preaching. However, Luke ends his book with the word "*freely*" *('akōlútōs),* and so a door remains open and gives us a basis for hope (28:30–31).

I do not claim that the previous discussion exhausts all the possibilities of our theme. A detailed examination of Pauline theology, for example, surely would produce even more enriching perspectives. Furthermore, much of the theme's complexity stems from a question that still awaits a clear answer. As Segundo reminds us:

> What is the exact relationship between, for example, the revelation of Jesus in the New Testament and the revelation of God in the Old Testament? Though it may seem hard to believe, the fact is that this basic and important question has scarcely been given a clear answer over the past twenty centuries of Christian living. And that fact has conditioned the whole of theology.[38]

I agree wholeheartedly, but I insist that the obvious continuity between the Old and New Testament teaching about oppression (James, etc.) permits us to draw the following conclusion: *according to biblical theology, the main cause of poverty is oppression.* When New Testament writers introduce complementary perspectives (the devil, powers, healings as liberation, persecution as a form of oppression, etc.), by no means do they intend to deny such a basic Old Testament teaching.

If this conclusion is correct, there are enormous implications for the church's proclamation of the good news to the poor and for its entire ministry. Especially in countries dominated by a capitalist ideology and mentality, we are faced with a tremendous task of unmasking hoary prejudices. Without doing that we can never claim to fulfill the prophetic duty of pointing out the forms sin takes in the modern world (Eph. 5:11).[39] Nevertheless we also must emphasize that the New Testament church's glory and privilege is to live and proclaim the good news of God's kingdom. This kingdom is God's solution to the problem of poverty, foreshadowed in the Year of Jubilee (Lev. 25; Luke 4:19) and put into practice by the church in Acts as a foretaste of the kingdom's consummation.

In the law and the prophets we discover a terrifying exposé of the oppressive mechanisms that produce poverty.[40] In the gospel Jesus reveals that he came to "fulfill"—not to ignore—the law and the prophets. For that reason our gospel must respond to the problems of poverty and oppression; we must not pretend that poverty does not exist or claim that it arises primarily for different reasons. This response is found above all in praxis (consider the Greek title of Acts: *Praxeis*). As Paul demonstrates in Galatians, not only the fulness, but the authenticity of the gospel here hangs in the balance. Justification by faith *must* come to expression in "good works," a commitment to the poor (Gal. 2:9-10; 5:6). If this does not happen, we are living and preaching "another gospel" (1:6-9).

Chapter 4

The Bible, the Reformation, and Liberation Theologies

Just as the Reformation earthquake shattered the status quo of the church in sixteenth-century Europe, so Latin America totters in a politico-religious upheaval unprecedented in the history of the continent. The Second Vatican Council (1961–64) gave an incredible impulse to serious Bible study in Catholic countries that traditionally had viewed the Bible as forbidden "Protestant propaganda" (so still read the signs in windows of countless homes in Costa Rica when I arrived there in 1963!). Decades of surging Protestant Pentecostal church growth were crowned in the late 1960s when pentecostal phenomena (tongues, interpretation, prophecy, healing) and dramatic Evangelical-type conversion experiences broke through into other Protestant churches and mushroomed within the Catholic Church itself. (In Costa Rica informed sources report that within the last decade the charismatic movement within the Catholic Church gained more adherents than all the Protestant groups had after a century of church growth; even the president of the country [1981] is known to be a Catholic charismatic.)

While thousands of Catholics and mainline Protestants were becoming charismatic, Medellín (1968) and Puebla (1979) focused world attention on the controversial new theologies of liberation surging up from new "ecclesial base communities" of poor believers throughout the continent. These *comunidades de base* and theologies of liberation struggled to realign a traditionally conservative church with the oppressed-poor in their struggle for survival. The prolonged tense struggle over the new Panama Canal treaty, the Sandinista revolution in Nicaragua that toppled the 40-year-old Somoza dynasty, and guerrilla wars in El Salvador and Guatemala focused world attention on the crisis in Central America.

The time has come when we must ask whether the politico-theologico-religious upheaval in Latin America is not of greater significance for the proper understanding and use of the Bible than is the Reformation itself. The Reformation, taking advantage of the scientific linguistic gains of the

61

Renaissance and the technological breakthrough of the printing press, taught
the churches to read the Bible from the perspective of the middle class (the new
bourgeoisie). The reformers and their successors thought of themselves as
doing what today we call "historico-grammatical exegesis," but in reality it
was more grammatical than historical, lacking both the sharper historical
dimension introduced by modern biblical studies and the socio-economic
perspective of the liberation theologies.[1]

In Latin America the *comunidades de base* and their theologies of liberation
are forcing us to undertake a new kind of exegesis that is more authentically
historical: *to read the Bible from the perspective of the oppressed-poor,* which
of course was the historical and socio-economic context of the people of God
(with very few exceptions) throughout Bible history.

Read in this way, major themes and structural elements of biblical theology
itself come into their own (most of them absent or strangely distorted in
traditional multitomed theological works—even those that seek to break with
the old systematic molds and call themselves "biblical"). Thus in all the
immense variety of liberation theologies we find certain biblical themes and
perspectives continually repeated (whether the rest of the theological package
consists mainly of traditional Evangelical affirmations or includes some
modern deviations). These dominant themes and structural elements include:

1) *Oppression* as the fundamental cause of poverty.
2) The *poor* as the primary focus of the church's praxis.
3) *Class struggle*, both as a socio-economic and ecclesiastical reality.[2]
4) *Agape-love* as a conflictive response.[3]
5) The paradigm of the *exodus* as the original revolution.[4]
6) Salvation biblically understood as integral *liberation*.[5]
7) The socio-economic dimension of *justice* seen as implying
   democratization in the ownership and control of the means of
   production.[6]
8) *Land* as the fundamental biblical substratum (agrarian society) for
   human life and economic productivity.[7]
9) The *wrath of God* as the appropriate response of indignation against
   oppression and injustice (expressed in prophetic proclamation of
   judgment).[8]
10) The socio-economic and political dimension in *christology* and
    ecclesiology (option for the poor given political expression).[9]
11) *Sanctification* (the Christian life) and *missiology* as involving option for
    and commitment to the oppressed-poor and revolutionary *praxis* (in
    place of the static Greek philosophical category of "ethics"), with all
    the problematic concerning legitimate force, violence, and pacifism.[10]
12) Christian *hope* as embracing the new person (2 Cor. 5:17); new earthly
    society (Eph. 1:10; Rev. 21–22); and a renewed earth and cosmos
    characterized by perfect justice and peace (Matt. 5:5; 2 Pet. 3:13;
    Rom. 8).[11]

In the present work I have focused particularly on the biblical teaching in the first two areas (oppression and the poor), but inevitably this has led me to mention other related spheres of biblical concern.

Few indeed are the biblical texts where proper attention to these themes and perspectives does not revolutionize our comprehension of the gospel and the Scriptures. The difference is certainly comparable to that between medieval allegorical commentaries (not to mention countless contemporary platonizing reruns) and the commentaries of Luther and Calvin. Even a superficial comparison of the biblical teaching emanating from the *comunidades de base* and theologies of liberation with traditional dogmatics and commentaries makes painfully clear the extent to which these latter have distracted attention from primary concerns of the text to involve us in controversies over trivialities and matters of secondary importance. Jesus perceived and denounced precisely this same tendency on the part of the politico-religious leaders of his own epoch when he said:

> You are careful to tithe even your spices—mint, dill, and cummin. But you have neglected the really important matters of the law—justice, mercy, and faithfulness. You should have practiced the latter without neglecting the former. You blind guides! You strain out a gnat and gulp down a camel [Matt. 23:23–24].

Ought we not to recognize the *comunidades de base* and their theologies of liberation as the authentic "fundamentalists"—those who call us back to perspectives and emphases that are really the fundamental ones in the Bible itself? They force us to face up to the basic questions—the kind that alone will be decisive at the final judgment (Matt. 25:31–46). Many Christians seek to evade the challenge by traditional escapisms: repeated "reconsecrations" to a Christ not attested to in the Scriptures; continual "seeking for God" in all the places where he has made clear he is not to be found; charismatic fervor that becomes a fever of interminable and ever multiplying religious services; evangelistic zeal that disintegrates into loveless proselytizing (Matt. 23:15); and dedication to Jonahlike missions that propel us—usually via jet—everywhere except the place God commanded.

Like Lazarus at the gate of Dives (Luke 16), the voices from the theologies of the oppressed poor emerging from slums and *campesino* groups throughout Latin America will not be accomplices to our favorite copouts. They force us to reconsider *who is* the *Christ* we propose to serve—a domesticated Jesus at the eternal service of colonizers, oppressors, and tyrants? *Where* and *how are we to seek God* according to the Scriptures—with ever multiplying worship services (Amos 5) and fasts (Isa. 58)? *Whom do we praise* in our prayers—the liberating, justice-establishing God of the exodus, or some capitalist/feudal idol, legitimizer and preserver of crass injustice, violence, and torture? *What is the gospel* we proclaim—an alienating opium or really good news of authentic liberation? *What is the* real *mission of the church* in dominated Latin

America—just to "save souls," be it by Protestant sermons or Catholic sacraments?

These questions and others like them are so fundamental that they represent nothing less than a call to conversion. Evangelical and charismatic Christians especially (probably because we have always thought of ourselves as the experts in calling everybody else to conversion) feel threatened and shaken by the new phenomenon.

No one was more defensive than I in my first encounter! When a young fellow professor in our seminary began to teach a course in "Latin American Theology" I became very defensive and considered it a case of incurable and fanatic nationalism. Did not our wonderful Christian systematic theologies point to a "deposit" (2 Tim. 1:14) of divine truth revealed once and for all as attested in the Bible? But on witnessing student euphoria with the new theology, in a fit of bad humor I tried calling my own course "Latin American Hebrew Grammar" (for some reason this tactic never produced comparable enthusiasm).

Now I find myself asking why in the world I reacted with such negative emotionalism to the new theological insights. Despite a reverential respect for the old masters of dogmatics (and still maintained in the form of critical appreciation), for years I had fully accepted and enthusiastically taught the plurality of contextualized biblical theologies. Even at Wheaton Graduate School of Theology in 1956 we were being taught to distinguish Pauline from Johannine from synoptic theology.

Finally a particular historical perspective enabled me to understand the typical "gringo culture-shock" at the new Latin American theologies. I call the perspective "The Reformation in Germany as seen from England." (The view from Costa Rica as taught in public schools was not much different when I arrived there in 1963!)

When the Reformation exploded in the cultural-economic "dogpatch" that was Germany in 1517, the English made no effort to conceal their repugnance and disgust ("Can something good come out of *Germany?*"). Immediately erudite English theologians began to attack the ridiculous extremes, point out patent errors, and expose the diabolical heresies that abounded on the continent. Young King Henry VIII offered himself to head up the charge with his sturdy defense of medieval sacramentarianism (*Assertio Septem Sacramentorum*, 1521). The English theologians spoke contemptuously of the "savage German boar" (Luther) and had no trouble at all finding plenty of ammunition for their war against the Lutheran apostasy. Preposterous blunders loomed on every horizon as easy targets.

For starters, Luther had broken his sacred vows and married a nun escaped from her convent. He had proceeded to call the book written by our Lord's own brother a "right strawy epistle" and sought to eliminate it from the canon (its only crime being its call for "good works"). Luther had inflamed German peasants with a lot of irresponsible rhetoric, and then with crude and abusive language he had called on the German nobles to stomp out the revolution with ferocious fits of violence that left thousands dead. The plunge into apostasy was finally crowned when Luther even approved the bigamous marriage of Philip of Hesse.

While Luther ran wild in Germany his erstwhile disciple Carlstadt devoted himself to destroying the priceless sacred art in the Christian churches, blasphemously calling it all "idolatry." Others (such as the Socinians) began to deny the doctrine of the Trinity and attack Anselm's works on the atoning death of Christ as "immoral and legalistic nonsense." Finally, a group of Anabaptists in Münster had begun to teach and practice polygamy and had thrown themselves into a disastrous armed revolution against the divinely instituted feudal regime. (Calvin, dolefully presiding over the burning of Servetus in Geneva, created less furor, because everyone knew that was how the Bible said heretics and witches were to be treated.)

How could one ever dream or pretend that in the midst of academic absurdities, diabolical heresy, or scandalous immorality God was at work producing the greatest revival of biblical Christianity in the history of the church? The English, at any rate, knew they had sufficient basis to call down the wrath of heaven on all responsible for the new developments.

Within a few years the Council of Trent had led the entire Catholic Church along the same route, pronouncing anathema upon the Reformation in not very guarded language: apostasy from the true faith. The doors slammed shut against the Lutheran heresies and remained bolted for more than four centuries, until Pope John XXIII managed to pry open some windows.

When the Latin American theological revolution began erupting in the late 1960s and early 1970s, many of us recently arrived from the United States felt something like a King George who had mistakenly stumbled in uninvited on the Boston Tea Party. The euphoria seemed insane. What respectable theologian could celebrate on seeing the combined wisdom of Augustine, Aquinas, Luther, Calvin, and Barth dumped merrily in the drink?

Now even so stern a critic of liberation theology as J. Andrew Kirk emphasizes its importance as:

> the first non-imitative theology to have sprung from the Third World nations; indeed the first creative theological thought to have arisen outside Europe or North America since the earliest years of the Church.

Although warning against many extremes, he commends the new theologies for "certainly struggling with the right kind of questions."[12] This is a far cry from initial conservative reactions ("another theological fad") and caricatures ("throw a hand grenade for Jesus")!

However, despite the entirely legitimate concerns of many to conserve all valid insights and gains of traditional orthodox (and neo-orthodox) theologies—whether Protestant or Catholic—we should not pretend that any of these historical alternatives can be structurally preserved by sewing on a patch of pentecostalism or liberationism. The theological revolution is too profound to permit such a superficial resolution. Should we try to dump all the new wine in the old skins, neither wine nor wineskin would be preserved, as Jesus warned us.

The faculty of our seminary came to realize this in the process of adopting our "Affirmation of Faith and Commitment" (1974). In this document, after much debate, we opted for liberation as the structurally vertebral element for our theology and praxis. Certainly, as even many of the most conservative biblical theologians now recognize, "liberation" is as defensible as any alternative to describe the leitmotif of biblical theology. Thus in a continent fundamentally characterized by domination and oppression as the primary concrete forms sin takes, it is entirely appropriate—and many of us would say essential—that the announcement of the good news, in praxis as well as verbal proclamation, should focus on liberation as the fundamental content (as it was in Jesus' own ministry and preaching, according to Luke 4:18–19). Within such a theology structured by oppression and liberation, historic biblical and theological truths may be conserved. But all are transformed when integrated into a biblical concern for liberation from oppression instead of the typical post-Constantinian ideological captivity (of which capitalism is only one of the latter-day expressions) that domesticates and instrumentalizes Christian truth and religion to preseve an unjust status quo.

Christian voices of the most diverse theological persuasions have agonized over the crisis of society and church in recent decades. Aleksandr Solzhenitsyn, in his famous Harvard commencement address "A World Split Apart" (1978), decries the rationalistic humanism, or humanistic autonomy, characteristic of both the U.S.S.R. and the U.S.A. that leaves us with no higher reference point.[13] Yale professor Brevard S. Childs as far back as 1970 found the mainline denominations suffering from a "biblical theology in crisis," and called for a radical reevaluation of higher criticism and a return to the values of the precritical commentaries that take seriously the canonical form and status of the biblical text.[14] Conservative-Evangelical theologian Carl F. H. Henry insists that the cries of authority can be solved only by recognition of an inerrant Bible.[15]

In Latin America neither analysis nor solutions from the First World seem applicable to the Third World situation. But our reading of the history of the church and of the history of biblical interpretation makes us grateful that at least there is some sense of crisis. Our own rather different reading of the crisis might well start from the response of the great nineteenth-century Baptist evangelist, Charles H. Spurgeon, who said, "Defend the Bible? I would prefer to defend a lion!"

Simply put, the post-Constantinian theological structures now diagnosed as "in crisis" all have this in common: they try to keep the lion in a cage. Always they want to teach the lion that it is not courteous to roar. Then, to resolve the crisis of authority, various tactics are suggested. One of the most recent is the creation of a special commission to proclaim, defend, and politically promote the theological doctrine of the "inerrancy" of the caged lion. But extreme inerrantists, like many higher critics, tend to become so absorbed by the "fern seed" that they fail to notice the "elephants."

From Latin America we have good news for our perplexed brethren from all theological camps: passing through this woefully "undeveloped" area, the lion managed to escape from his cage! Their "crisis of authority" is resolved:

> The Lion has roared;
>   who will not fear?
> The Lord God has spoken;
>   who can but prophesy? [Amos 3:8].

Of course a roaring lion running loose suffers extremely bad press coverage in certain circles—particularly among First World theologians. Some prefer to draw caricatures of the lion instead of listening to his roar. Others humbly seek to adjust their theological criteria to the lamentable new reality. They suggest, for instance, that although it is always wrong to roar (certainly discourteous and probably sinful!), they would be willing to listen from time to time if the lion just wants to growl a little against all the atrocities of the International Communist Conspiracy (always taking care, of course, not to mix up politics with religion). And of course they point out that it would be a scandalous lack of gratitude to roar against the capitalist system, because (according to their theology seven times purified from all ideological and political contamination) it is this that gives the lion his "food in due season" (Ps. 104:27, 21).

In Latin America the church has affirmed for more than four centuries the inerrancy of the Scriptures, the Trinity, the virgin birth of Christ, his full deity, propitiatory death, bodily resurrection, and second coming. But with what result? One, in which many take rather uncritical pride, is that conservative churches have higher growth rates. And so, according to certain statistics, we have more Christians than human beings in Latin America. Inexplicably, however, the continent continues to be a "mission field" whose urgent needs of all sorts are cause for concern by Catholic agencies as well as Protestant.

In the last decade, with a roaring lion on the rampage, many of our traditional theological preoccupations undoubtedly have become somewhat neglected with the press of more urgent tasks. Inevitably we have come to view the "crisis of authority" lamented by First World theologians in a very different light. We see it not as a crisis of authority, but rather as a kind of "crisis of hearing" (a failure repeatedly diagnosed in both Old and New Testaments).

C. S. Lewis might have put it this way. When two groups of persons respond with such diverse reactions as "The lion is roaring—who can but prophesy" and "Whatever shall we do about our crisis of authority?" there are only two possibilities: one group is crazy or the others are deaf. First World theologians, having proceeded for more than a decade on the first assumption only to find their crisis deepening, might try working for a while from the second hypothesis.

Occasionally some of those deranged Latin American theologians sit down and begin to exchange impressions about the "crisis of hearing" (as they see it) up north. At first some argued it was just a language barrier. The lion, aside from his unpardonable lack of courtesy and gratitude, had such an incredibly bad sense of public relations that he started roaring in Spanish and Portuguese—even when no interpreter was present! Had he, in a moment of forgetfulness, merely lapsed into German or French—or even Polish!—things might have been patched up with a few explanatory press releases. But he stubbornly persisted in roaring on and on in Spanish or Portuguese. And even when present, the translators could not begin to keep up with the continual torrent of roaring, and so a lot of misunderstandings resulted.

Of course even from the beginning a few First World theologians of very different theological persuasions began to realize what had happened and went around insisting "They're not crazy—we've been deaf!" In Latin America at first no one could figure out why in the world these few were able to hear the lion's roar when almost everyone else seemed to be deaf. It only complicated the problem. No common theological criterion could be identified to explain the phenomenon. Then one of the oldest and wisest (one of the first to alert us to the lion's roar) journeyed long in the lands suffering the crisis of authority and saw why. "Every Christian," he said, "who is actually working to help the oppressed-poor recognizes immediately the voice of the lion's roar. But the vast majority in affluent societies never have any personal contact with the poor and never struggle in practical ways to help free them, so they can't hear anything." We all recalled again how true was the word given to the brother of our Lord:

> Religion that God our Father accepts as pure and faultless is this: to go visit orphans and widows in their oppression and to keep oneself from being polluted by the Consumer Society [James 1:29].

And we thought, too, about the experiences of the Prophet Amos, the very first in Israel to try to reduce to writing what he understood of the lion's roar:

> Then Amaziah the priest of Bethel sent a message to Jeroboam king of Israel: "Amos is raising a conspiracy against you in the very heart of Israel. The land cannot bear all his words. . . . [Obviously he had completely misunderstood what Amos was trying to say!] Then Amaziah said to Amos, "Clear out of here, you seer! Go back south to Judah. Earn your bread there and do your prophesying there. But do not prophesy anymore at Bethel, because this is the king's sanctuary and the temple of the kingdom" [Good priests like Amaziah were always careful never to mix up politics with their religion.] [Amos 7:10–14].

Unfortunately Amos never tells us what actually happened to Amaziah—or himself—after this encounter. We do not know whether Amaziah dedicated his remaining years to a multivolume treatise on the inerrancy of the torah, or the crisis in sacerdotal theology, or simply began to bewail the terrible silence of God. But this we know:

> Jesus said to the doctor of theology, "Go thou and do likewise" [Luke 10:37].

> [Then Jesus said] "He who has an ear, let him hear what the Spirit says to the churches" [Rev. 2:7, 11, 17, 29; 3:6, 13, 22; cf. Luke 8:8].

> And as you walk your ears shall hear a word behind you, saying, "This is the way, walk in it," when you turn to the right or when you turn to the left [Isa. 30:21].

> In that day the deaf shall hear the words of a book
> and out of their gloom and darkness
> the eyes of the blind shall see.
> The meek shall obtain fresh joy in the Lord,
> and the poor among men shall exult in the Holy One of Israel.
> [Isa. 29:18–19].

PART THREE

PROPHETIC PERSPECTIVES
AND THE
GOSPEL OF THE POOR

Chapter 5

The Oppressed Servant:
A *Relectura* of Isaiah 52:13–53:12 from
Latin America

The historical situation addressed in Isaiah's fourth Servant Song has a great deal in common with contemporary Latin America, where two powerful empires struggle to dominate weaker nations. Some conservative scholars continue to argue that the entire canonical book stems from one Isaiah, living in the eighth century B.C., but directing his message in chapters 40–55 to a situation about 150 years later. Even by this reckoning, however, the historical situation addressed remains the same: Israel in exile in Babylonia ca. 550 B.C. with the Persian empire under Cyrus on the horizon and promising "liberation."[1]

Claus Westermann represents common scholarly opinion when he says that the fourth Song of the Servant is "probably the work of a disciple of Second Isaiah."[2] Most scholars do not dismiss the possibility that Second Isaiah was its author, but the fourth song presents a highly developed theology of suffering with a vocabulary considerably different from the previous songs.[3] Furthermore, this song breaks abruptly into the book's context at this point. Connections with the context appear to be more of contrast than of continuity.

The main body of this fourth song appears to be an individual psalm of thanksgiving (or "declarative psalm of praise") that tells of oppression (53:2–9) and liberation (10–11a). Still the song differs from this psalm type in three ways: (1) The narrator is not the one who suffers; instead a group ("we") reports the story of suffering in the third person. (2) Those who report the Servant's oppression and liberation have themselves experienced liberation because of the Servant's own sufferings. (3) In the psalms, the suffering that is reported always has clear limits; this song, however, tells us of an entire life (he grew, he suffered, he died, he was exalted).[4] In the first Servant Song God speaks; in the second and third songs the Servant speaks. However, in this fourth song we have something more complex and dramatic: first God speaks of his Servant (52:13-15); then the group that calls itself "we" speaks (53:1-11a); and God concludes the song (53:11b-12).

According to most scholars, the development and complexity of this song confirm that it was composed by a different author. If either First or Second Isaiah wrote it, it shows a great change in his thought and style, and would have to be dated to a later part of his life.[5] Second Isaiah is believed to have preached in Babylon between the first victories of Cyrus in 550 B.C. and the edict of liberation in 538 B.C. that permitted the first returns from captivity. Most scholars now date the fourth song after Second Isaiah's death.

ISAIAH 52:13-53:12, THE OPPRESSED SERVANT

52:13 [Yahweh announces:]
    Watch out! My Servant is going to win out by following my
        wisdom;
      he'll be high and lifted up and greatly exalted.
  14 Just as many were awestruck at him
      (so monstrously disfigured was his appearance
      and his form beyond human recognition)
  15 —that way he will sprinkle many nations—
    Rulers will shut their mouths before him,
    Because what no one ever told them they will see,
      and what they never heard they'll understand.
53:1 [Israel responds:]
    No one wants to believe our report;
      no one discerns the Liberator's arm in action.
  2 For he grew up before Him like a tender shoot,
      from arid earth, like a twisted root.
    He had neither beauty nor charisma that we should admire,
      and nothing in his appearance that we should desire.
  3 Despised and rejected by people,
      he was pain personified and always getting sick;
    Like someone people turn away from in embarrassment,
      he was despised—so we just reckoned him of no account!
  4 Nevertheless, turns out it was our sickness he'd picked up,
      and our pains that he carried off,
    Yet we took him for some kind of leper,
      scourged by God and humiliatingly oppressed *('anah)*.
  5 But he was pierced for our rebellion,
      oppressively crushed *(daka')* for our iniquity;
    The punishment that brought us prosperity fell on him,
      and his wounds meant healing for us.
  6 All of us, like sheep, got lost
      because each of us set his face to find his own way;

So the Liberator had to load on him
the punishment all of us deserve.

7 Like some animal, he was oppressively driven *(nagas)*,
really humiliatingly oppressed *('anah)*,
but not once did he open his mouth;
he was led away like a little lamb to the slaughterhouse;
and as a ewe stands mute before her shearers,
he never even opened his mouth.

8 By judicial oppression *('otser)* he was abducted,
as has become the custom;
but for his contemporaries—who even notices?
So he just disappeared from the land of the living.
Because of the rebellion of my people the blow fell on him.

9 So they fixed him up a grave among the wicked,
prepared his tomb with the rich,
Even though he never imitated their violence,
never even mentioned deception or dirty tricks.

10 Yet the Liberator purposed his crushing oppression *(daka')*,
and intended to let him get sick,
Only thus could he sacrifice his life to turn away divine
indignation,
then see his offspring and prolong his days!
Thus would the Liberator's purpose prosper by his hand.

11 [Yahweh explains:]
After all his soul's painful labor
he'll witness the dawn of liberation and be satisfied;
By his wise comprehension of my ways
my Just Servant will win acquittal for the masses,
since he himself suffers the consequences for their iniquities.

12 Therefore will I allot him an inheritance to share with the masses,
and he'll distribute the spoil among the strong,
Because he poured out his soul to death
and was treated like one of the rebels;
That way he took away the guilt of the masses,
and interposed as mediator for the rebels.

My translation is partly literalistic (to catch the precise vocabulary of
oppression and sickness) and partly paraphrastic (to catch certain overtones of
atonement and liberation). It should be compared with the excellent efforts in
such recent versions as NIV, JB, and NEB to appreciate the many possibilities
suggested by the provocative Hebrew original. My paraphrastic "dawn of
liberation" (53:11; cf. the NIV paraphrastic "light [of life]") is an attempt to
pair the themes of life and liberation, both of which are suggested by the
context.

THE PENTECOSTAL PERSPECTIVE:
SICKNESS AND HEALING

The Twelfth Article of the Assemblies of God concisely expresses the Pentecostal doctrine of "divine healing": "Deliverance from sickness is provided for in the atonement, and is the privilege of all believers (Isa. 53:3-4; Matt. 8:16-17)."[6] By basing themselves on this doctrine, Pentecostal churches have long conducted evangelistic healing campaigns as a basic strategy for growth in Latin America. Of course this emphasis has elicited certain criticisms, especially when it has gone to the extreme of criticizing those who are not cured for supposedly lacking faith.[7]

Perhaps partly in fear of such an extreme, most translations of the Isaian fourth song have not emphasized the sickness and its cure as forcefully as does the Hebrew in the passage. L. Alonso Schökel's translation is something of an exception: it renders verse 4: "we consider him a leper, wounded and humiliated by God."[8] This translation follows the Vulgate and Bernard Duhm's hypothesis (1892). Besides postulating the distinction between second and third Isaiah, and isolating the four Songs of the Servant, Duhm concluded that the the Servant described in the fourth song was a leprous rabbi.[9]

Duhm's hypothesis that the Servant suffered leprosy or some similar sickness is well supported by the Hebrew text. As an alternate reading to the RSV has it in verse 4a: "Surely he has borne our sickness *(holi)* and carried our pains *(mac'ob)*." Many translations obscure these terms but these same words occur in verse 3b where we should translate: "man of pains, acquainted with sickness," because the word *holi* simply means "sickness."[10]

Spiritualization began as early as the Septuagint. It translated Isaiah 53:4a: "He bore our sins *(hamartías)*." We can see how faulty that translation is when we realize that throughout the rest of the LXX *holi* is never translated "sin."[11] When Matthew quotes the text he breaks with the spiritualizing LXX and translates: "He took up our infirmities and carried diseases (NIV)." Despite the clear meaning of the Hebrew and Matthew's own authority, Christian translations have tended to avoid the literal meaning. One recent exception is John L. McKenzie's translation in the Anchor Bible. However, NEB uses "suffering" in 3b and 4a; RSV uses "grief(s)"; NIV uses "suffering" in 3b and "infirmities" in 4a. Thus, even though the Hebrew explicitly says that the Servant suffered sickness, Christian translations avoid the literal meaning, probably because they are influenced by the gospels that do not tell of any sickness that Jesus himself suffered. Perhaps also because they fear pentecostal extremes.

Another word used in Isaiah 53:3, 4 is *mac'ob,* which the NEB translates "tormented" and "torments"; the RSV and NIV, "sorrows." Because of its connection with *holi* we ought to understand the word in its primary meaning of physical pain and not as some emotional distress.

Words that more strongly suggest the Servant suffered from leprosy are the verb *naga'* ("to touch, wound," KB², p. 593) in 53:4c and the related noun *nega'* ("blow, plague," KB², p. 593) in 53:8d. The translation "leprosy" here is justified for the noun: of some 70 uses in the Old Testament, 54 occur in Leviticus 13 and 14 where they refer explicitly to leprosy.

In addition to the choice of words, the text suggests a leprosylike sickness when it describes others' reactions to the Servant. In 52:14, we read:

> As many were astonished at him—
> his appearance was so marred beyond human semblance,
> and his form beyond that of the sons of men (RSV).

Furthermore 53:3 says "and as one from whom men hide their faces." As a poem, the song does not explicitly say that the Servant was a leper. But because the vocabulary is heavily charged with words related to sickness (particularly leprosy) and to descriptions of human repugnance, a sickness similar to leprosy strongly suggests itself.

The final reference to the Servant's sickness occurs in 53:10a where the text literally says "but it pleased Yahweh to crush him, to make him sick" (*heheli*, hiphil perfect of *hl* or *hlh*; KB², pp. 298, 300). The verb *hlh* is related to the noun *holi*, which is translated "sickness" in verses 3b and 4a.

Besides the vocabulary suggesting sickness, we find that the healing of the people occurred as a result of the Servant's sicknesses: "and with his wounds we have been healed *(rapha')*" (53:5b).[12]

In summary we can say that in the fourth Servant Song we find at least six words for sickness and healing (not counting *shalom*) that appear a total of eight times. In addition we have three lines—52:14b,c, and 53:3c—that show how others react to someone who is seriously ill and disfigured. Thus, when Matthew (8:17) translates the Hebrew of Isaiah 53:4 literally and relates the "sick healer" Servant to Jesus in his ministry of healing the sick, Matthew does not focus on a secondary element in describing the Servant; instead he is dealing with a primary feature. We may even say that Matthew found additional evidence that Jesus fulfilled the prophecy precisely where the modern reader finds it most difficult to do so. "Fulfillment" in the New Testament, of course, is not always to be equated with historico-grammatical exegesis of the original text.

Whatever the case, we have no reason to doubt that the Pentecostal doctrine of healing as part of the gospel is profoundly rooted in the Servant's sufferings and that this finds adequate foundation in the Hebrew text of the fourth song. Surely one can go to extremes in mass Pentecostal healing campaigns, but Isaiah 53 and Matthew 8:17 do not give us the liberty of going to the other extreme of removing from our gospel the ministry to heal the sick.[13] Edward J. Young acknowledges the literal sense of the Hebrew about the sickness in Isaiah 53, but then maintains that the word "sickness" represents sin.[14] Such a spiritualization does not take into account the synthetic character of Hebrew thought or the background of the blessings and curses of the covenant (Deut.

28; Lev. 26). In the fourth song the Servant's work makes it possible for persons once more to enjoy all the blessings that the covenant promises. As the psalmist says, it is Yahweh who "forgives all your iniquities, who heals all your diseases" (Ps. 103:3).

THE EVANGELICAL TRADITION: PENAL SUBSTITUTION/FORENSIC JUSTIFICATION

What I mean by "evangelical tradition" is not limited to historical Protestantism; it includes evangelical elements in the Catholic tradition: Augustine, Anselm, Thomas Aquinas, and others. Their interpretations of the fourth Song of the Servant have so much in common with Protestant thought that it is not necessary to treat them separately here. Jon Sobrino and other critics of the evangelical theology of the atonement give the impression that St. Anselm invented this doctrine. However, more careful studies point to its roots in the church fathers.[15] We find this teaching in St. Augustine *(Enchiridion),*[16] and further developed in Luther,[17] Calvin,[18] and Wesley.[19]

Furthermore, the evangelical tradition includes the great confessions and catechisms especially of the Reformation period: *Heidelberg Catechism*, questions and answers 12–18; the *Thirty-Nine Articles* of the Anglican Church, Article 31; Luther's *Larger Catechism*, the Creed: Article 1; cf. *Westminster Confession,* VII:5. In the modern era this doctrine is confirmed by such neo-orthodox theologians as Karl Barth[20] and Emil Brunner,[21] conservative evangelicals such as Donald G. Bloesch and G. C. Berkouwer,[22] and also Wolfhart Pannenberg.[23] Exegetes such as Leon Morris[24] and C.E.B. Cranfield[25] support them.

The Human Problem

The evangelical tradition contributes significantly to interpreting the fourth song by insisting that the root of the human problem is sin. Old Testament covenant theologies (Lev. 26 and Deut. 28) confirm the evangelical conviction that Israel's major problem in Babylonian exile was not the captivity itself but the apostasy that caused it. Thus in Isaiah 40–55 the primary solution is not liberation from Babylon but redemption from sin. The major concern is not the return to Palestine but the return to God. Nevertheless when we study the theology of sin and repentance in this context we can see that the traditional evangelical vision, despite its many valid elements, does not adequately understand the fourth song's teaching on this theme.

In the first place, the word that the author prefers to describe the human problem in Isaiah 53 is not "sin" (*ḥata'*, 12c "he bore our sin"), but rather "rebellion" *(pesha').* This is a political term that expresses how an individual or nation rebels and thus breaks the solidarity of an alliance or an agreement:

he was wounded for our rebellions [53:5a] . . .
he was wounded for the rebellions of his/my people [8d] . . .

and he was counted among the rebels [12d] . . .
and he interceded for the rebels [12f].

The other word that the author prefers to describe the human dilemma is
"iniquity" *('awon)*, the perverse twistedness resulting from rebellion. This
word occurs three times:

he was wounded for our iniquities [5b] . . .
and the Lord laid on him the iniquity of us all [6d] . . .
and he shall bear their iniquities [11c].

In addition to the explicit words *pesha', 'awon,* and *hata',* the human
problem is described with the image of stupid, stubborn, and dispersive sheep:

and we like sheep have gone astray *(ta'ah)*
and we have turned everyone to his own way [6ab].

Thus the extreme individualism often extolled as the foundation of a
"Christian (i.e., capitalist) economy" the fourth song here considers a root
cause of the human problem.[26]

In order adequately to understand how the fourth song analyzes the human
problem, we must ask *who* are the guilty ones. The song speaks basically of two
groups without expressly identifying them: the "many" and "we." When we
analyze these terms we find an answer that clarifies the message of the song.

The "many" *(rabbim)* only occurs when God speaks: in the introduction
and in the conclusion of the song. It is used first in 52:14a: "as many were
astonished at him" [the Servant]. The context suggests that this refers to the
gentile nations: we read in 52:15a: "so he shall sprinkle many nations *(goyim
rabbim)*."

When God speaks in the conclusion, the song again refers to the "many":

My Servant will justify many *(rabbim)*
and he shall bear their iniquities [11cd].
Therefore, I will divide him a portion with the many *(rabbim);* RSV,
"great") . . .
Yet he bore the sin of many *(rabbim)* [12ae].

Thus God's speaking in the song's introduction and conclusion stresses the
universality of the Servant's work.[27]

Nevertheless, in the body of the song (53:1–10, esp. 1–6) another group
speaks: "we." Who are they? Could they be the very nations that speak of
Israel as the Servant who suffers on their account? As Delitzsch points out,
usually when a "we" bursts into some kind of prophecy it refers to Israel
(42:24; 64:5; 16:6; 24:16).[28] In the context we find a contrast between the
nations (ignorant and dumb, 52:15) and the "we" (eyewitnesses, but also

lacking discernment, 53:1–4). This contrast makes it impossible to equate the two groups. Verse 8 further confirms the identification of the "we" group as Israel: "For he was cut off from the land of the living, stricken for the rebellions of my/his people." Let it be noted that if Israel is speaking here as "we," it cannot also be the Servant.

Among the group of "we" there were no exceptions:

> All we like sheep have gone astray.
> We have turned everyone his own way;
> and Yahweh has laid on him the guilt of all of us [53:6].

Thus, in this context Israel confesses to be just as rebellious as the nations, but God announces that because of the Servant's work the nations will be sprinkled just as Israel (52:15, NIV).

The question arises whether the Servant sinned. Mowinckel insists that the Servant must have sinned because in Old Testament thought there was no such thing as a human being without sin.[29] The song calls him just (53:11c; or "righteous," RSV) and says in verse 9cd: "he had done no violence and there was no deceit in his mouth." But we may interpret these expressions in a relative manner. Nevertheless, two factors suggest that the Servant did live without sinning (or at least allow that as a real possibility):

(a) The sharp contrast between the Servant and "all we" (53:6).

(b) His sacrifice (10c) and substitution for sinners (53:4–6). How could the Servant die vicariously for sinners if he himself were guilty? The animal sacrifices in the Old Testament had to be "without blemish."

Penal Substitution

The fourth song analyzes the basic human problem as rebellion, egotism, individualism, breaking of the covenant's solidarity, separation and alienation of all members from the community. This is the universal problem that affected both Israel ("we") and the rest of the nations ("the many"). What did God and his Servant do to counteract all that? In brief the answer that the fourth song gives consists of a series of affirmations, allusions, and images that we can summarize by saying that the Servant identifies himself with the rebellious and alienated, and suffers in their place the punishment and divine judgment they deserve.

First, we see this in the sober affirmations of 53:5, 6:

> He was wounded for our rebellions,
> crushed for our iniquities
> He bore the punishment *(musar)* that brought us peace
> and with his wounds we have been healed. . . .
> Yahweh laid on him the guilt of all of us.

It cannot be denied that these verses interpret the Suffering Servant's work in terms of penal substitution. As Westermann says, the Servant bore the sins of others and "the punishment that resulted from them."[30]

The meaning of the death of the Servant is further confirmed when we read in verse 10: "he makes himself *(nefesh)* a guilt offering *('asham)*." Why did the author of the song choose the term "guilt offering" to express the meaning of the Servant's death? Much has been written attempting to clarify the meaning of this *'asham* sacrifice in the Old Testament and also to distinguish it from the rest of the sacrifices, especially the sacrifice for sin (Lev. 4) with which it shares many characteristics. Without detailing all the interpretations, we can say that *'asham* is precisely the word to use here because the priest always offered the *'asham* when he declared a leper cleansed or after he had sprinkled the blood of a sacrificed animal (Lev. 14:7, 12–17, 21, 24–29).[31] The *'asham* sacrifice is also appropriate because it assures pardon even in the case of sins committed unconsciously (cf. the stupid sheep in Isa. 53:6).[32] Additionally, the *'asham* sacrifice is a compensation that highlights the complete satisfaction for sin.[33] Thus, there are abundant theological reasons that might explain the reference to the *'asham* sacrifice. Nevertheless, poetic grounds may also explain the author's word choice. The result is a verse of exceptional beauty in Hebrew: *im-tasim 'asham-nafsho.*

The *'asham* sacrifice was a propitiatory sacrifice, as were all the sacrifices in Leviticus 1–5 (cf. Num. 1:53; 16:46; 18:5).[34] It was the sacrifice in response to God's anger mentioned various times in a broader context (Isa. 43:13, 15; 37:6; 48:9; 51:17, 20, 22; 54:8, 9; cf. 34:2). Maximiliano García Cordero rightly concludes that "all the sufferings of the Servant were supposed to placate divine anger."[35]

That the Servant's death is correctly interpreted as penal substitution is also confirmed by the texts that say that he "bore the sins" of many. The conclusion to the song explicitly states this:

> By his knowledge my just Servant will justify many *(sabal)*,
> and he will bear their guilt [53:11 cd; cf. 4a]. . . .
>
> he was counted *(manah,* nifal) with the rebels
> yet he carried *(nasa'*; cf. v. 4a) the sin of many.
> and he interceded *(paga',* hifil; cf. 6c) for the rebels [12def].

We can compare these explicit expressions with other similar statements:

> Surely he has borne *(nasa')* our sicknesses
> and has carried *(sabal)* our pains [4ab].
>
> He was wounded *(halal)* for our rebellions,
> He was crushed *(daka')* for our guilt.

> Upon him was the punishment *(musar)* that brought us peace
> and with his stripes we have been healed [5].

> Yahweh laid *(paga', hifil)* on him
> the iniquity of us all [6cd].

> He was stricken *(nega')* for the rebellions of my/his people [8d].

> But it pleased Yahweh to crush him *(daka'),*
> he made him sick [10ab].

The New Testament repeats this concept of bearing sins for the others (1 Pet. 2:24; Heb. 9:29). Several authors emphasize that the obvious Old Testament meaning is "to suffer the punishments and consequences of sin"[36]—that is, "to suffer the penal consequences of sin and its curse, which is separation from God."[37] Exegetes refer to various Old Testament texts that clearly demonstrate this meaning: Numbers 14:33, 34; 18:1; Ezekiel 18:20; Deuteronomy 21:23 (cf. Gal. 3:13); Exodus 28:38; Numbers 18:1 Leviticus 24:15, 16; etc.

Forensic Justification

As we have said, the evangelical tradition has defined rebellion against God as the basic human problem. Consequently the Servant's work as penal substitution is set forth as the heart of God's answer to the problem.[38] Evangelicals insist that the fourth song teaches forensic justification as a basic aspect of the Servant's work. Similarly, in the history of theology Anselm's exposition of atonement theology prepared the way for Luther's understanding of justification. In Isaiah 53 the text may be literally translated:

> Because of his knowledge my just servant will justify *(yatsdiq,*
>   hifil) many
> and [or "because"] he will bear their iniquities [11bc].

Modern translations support this interpretation, although the Jersualem Bible omits the word "just," considering it repetitious. Such variations, supported by many authorities, do not affect the basic meaning of justification here.

Mowinckel and Westermann, however, propose a very different interpretation: "My servant will stand forth as righteous before the many."[39] The LXX and the Soncino Jewish commentary offer similar translations.[40] Mowinckel and Westermann say that we should understand the hifil of *tsdq* in this context as an internal causative. Furthermore, they quote Isaiah 50:7, 8, in which God justifies the Servant: "The one who justifies me *(matsdiqi,* hifil, participle) is near." Obviously Isaiah 50:8 speaks of *God's* action in justifying his Servant, but 53:11c may well introduce a complementary truth—that is, the *Servant's* action that justifies "the many." This interpretation agrees better with the parallel line, 53:11d: "and/because he shall bear their iniquities." Furthermore, the hifil is commonly a causative verb and an "internal" hifil is very rare.[41]

The forensic sense of justification is also preferable because of the priestly context of the chapter: the priests pronounce lepers cleansed; reference is made to the *'asham* sacrifice; and the action of sprinkling the nations is also mentioned.[42] If we understand 53:11cd this way, it complements the teaching of penal substitution by affirming the justification of the guilty, which Young rightly calls a "glorious interchange."[43] We may compare the repeated assurances of pardon in Isaiah 40–55 (40:2; 43:25; 44:22; 55:6, 7; cf. 47:11) with the more profound elaboration here in the fourth song.

Conclusion

The concerns that evangelical theology has emphasized do not exhaust the meaning of the fourth song. Nevertheless, although we gladly accept what Pentecostalism and liberation theologies offer by way of complement, we should not reject what has meant so much for the Christian faith throughout the ages. Despite the efforts of liberal rationalistic theologies to deny and weaken it, the element of penal substitution in the Servant's death stands more strongly confirmed than ever.

Throughout the centuries the greatest preachers have known that if they wanted to "speak to the heart of Jerusalem" (Isa. 40:2), they had to emphasize this truth. The element of penal substitution has inspired most of the great hymns about Christ's death, even when it is not stated explicitly—thus Isaac Watts's "When I Survey the Wondrous Cross." The importance of this doctrine in Christian theology, historical piety, and evangelism may be explained in part because of the following factors:

1) It emphasizes (as biblical theology always has) the divine attributes of perfect justice and righteousness (Rom. 3:24–26)[44] and holiness. Precisely these characteristics are essential for developing a valid contextual theology in Latin America.

2) We appreciate more not only God's justice, but also divine love when we realize that the Servant suffered hell—that is, separation from God—in our place. Thus when John seeks to expound the depths of divine love he must refer to the propitiation of divine anger: "This is love: not that we loved God, but that he loved us and sent his son as a propitiation for our sins" (1 John 4:10).

3) We can understand better both the seriousness of sin and God's righteous indignation in response to sin wherever we encounter these elements in Scripture.

4) As Anselm saw so clearly, only thus can we understand the need for both the incarnation and death of God's Son. Jon Sobrino has complained that this

theory "knows far too much."[45] But it does not claim to know more than the Scriptures affirm. "The secret things belong to the Lord our God; but the things that are revealed belong to us and to our children forever, that we may do all the words of the law" (Deut. 29:29). We cannot deny this interpretation of the death of the Servant without denying what the Scriptures clearly teach.

Surely the history of theology and preaching and popular piety have taught us that there are dangers in this doctrine (as there are in any doctrine) and extremes that we must avoid. The Pentecostal and liberationist perspectives help us flesh out the doctrine and avoid certain dangers and extremes. But they cannot supplant the historical evangelical doctrine, or deny its importance for any Latin American theology that seeks to be biblical.

"HE WILL SPRINKLE"

The meaning of the Servant's death becomes clear in the climactic statement in 52:15a: "So he shall sprinkle *(yazzeh,* from *nazah)* many nations."[46] Commentaries and translations, despite the clarity of the Hebrew text, have rendered this in many different ways. In order for us to understand the meaning of the Servant's work when he "sprinkles" the nations, we need only recall the priestly circles in which the author of the fourth song moved:

1) He explains the Servant's work by saying that he gives his life (*nephesh*, something that includes blood, Lev. 17:11) as a propitiatory sacrifice to remove guilt (*'asham*; cf. Lev. 5:14–26; 7:1–7; 14:14–31, etc.).

2) As we have noted, the fourth song employs words associated with sicknesses, especially leprosy, in describing the Servant. Of the 22 uses of *nazah* (sprinkle) in the Old Testament, 15 are in Leviticus, where sprinkling persons or things with blood, water, or oil is a frequent theme (thus the leper in 14:7).[47] We find four other similar uses in Numbers (8:7; 19:4, 18, 19). Besides these uses and those in Isaiah (52:15; 63:3), *nazah* occurs only in 2 Kings 9:33.

3) The Servant's task "to justify" *(tsdq)* also finds its roots in the priestly context. This is precisely von Rad's point when he expounds the priestly function in declaring persons such as lepers clean or unclean (Lev. 14:7).[48]

4) The immediate context of the fourth song—a call for separation and departure from Babylon—is couched in priestly terms:

> Depart, go out thence,
> touch no unclean thing;
> go out from the midst of her, purify yourselves,
> you who bear the vessels of the Lord [52:11].

5) The Servant is compared to a sacrificial lamb, probably the paschal lamb for the new exodus.

Thus, despite many modern translations, there are strong arguments in favor of the Hebrew meaning "sprinkle." Although the LXX here reads "will be astonished" *(thaumasontai)*, the authority of the MT is reinforced by the

Dead Sea Scrolls (IQIs[ab]), the *Manual of Discipline* (iv, 21; cf. iii, 1), Aquila, and the Syriac. Edward J. Young, James Muilenberg,[49] Gerhard von Rad,[50] the Koehler and Holladay lexicons, and C.-H. Hunzinger's article "*rantidzo, rantismos*"[51] are among the modern authorities that support "will sprinkle" as the best translation.

Besides the LXX testimony, the only weighty argument against the literal meaning of the MT is that one might expect an expression parallel with 52:15b: "Kings shall shut their mouths before him." But if we were to accept the LXX reading in order to establish parallelism between 15a and 15b, we break the parallelism with 14a, thus solving one problem by creating another. As Young has shown, the Hebrew syntax and poetic structure are more complex here.[52] If we follow the MT and respect the Hebrew syntax, we can translate literally:

52:14a Since *(ka'asher)* many were aghast at you [protasis]
    b (so *[ken]* disfigured more than man was his appearance
    c and his form more than the sons of men)
  15a —So *(ken)* he will sprinkle many nations—
    b kings will shut their mouths before him [apodosis].
    c For what *(ki'asher)* was not told to them they will see
    d and what *(wa'asher)* they did not see they will understand.

Although most of the verses in this song contain parallel pairs, 52:14–15 is not the only exception. Verses 7 and 11 also show some irregularities, with verse 7–8a giving us a similar pattern, a kind of inclusion: 7a parallel with 8a; 7b with 7e; 7c with 7d. The sandwichlike construction is further rounded off by the double repetition of "what" *('asher)* in 52:15cd, referring back to *'asher* in 14a: *ka'asher . . . ki'asher . . . wa'asher*. Perhaps 14bc and 15a represent inspired interpretive notes successively added to the song.

LIBERATION THEOLOGIES AND JUDAISM: OPPRESSION-LIBERATION

Of course there are many differences between Judaism and liberation theologies. Nevertheless, in interpreting the fourth song, it is helpful to treat the two together. They share many concerns and points of view, especially the concern to interpret the Old Testament texts historically, not taking into account the questions and perspectives foisted on it by Greek philosophy or arising later in the New Testament.

The Servant and Israel

Among the Jews after the time of Christ, the interpretation of the Servant as a collectivity prevailed, but an older Jewish tradition understood the Servant in the fourth song as the Messiah: LXX, Palestinian Targum on Isaiah 53, various rabbis.[53] It is clear that the Servant of the fourth song becomes a *person* and—from its author's perspective—a *future* person.[54] However, the collective interpretation still holds weight: it counteracts excessively individualistic interpretations of the song that would completely divorce the Servant from Israel and the people's history. The song points to self-centered individualism as the essence of sin (53:6), and liberation theologies warn us against the Greek tendency of creating dichotomies where God has established vital unities.

The final form of Isaiah 40–55 forbids us to conceive of the Servant as someone unrelated to Israel. The word "servant" *('ebed)* is a favorite term in this section, occurring 21 times. Outside the fourth song the word always refers to Israel—or to the faithful remnant (in two verses, 49:5, 6). In Isaiah 56–66 the word "servant" occurs 10 times, 9 of which refer to Israel (in 55:6 it refers to proselytes). In the fourth song itself, the Servant grows up among "us" as a "tender shoot" *(yoneq)* of a fallen tree (the exiled nation), 53:2; cf. 6:13; 11:1; Jer. 23:5, 6. He is described as a "root out of arid earth," a reference that firmly places the Servant among his exiled people (44:1–3).

Christian theology, insisting on Christ's deity, has no trouble believing that *one* person (being both God and man) is able to suffer condemnation and punishment for the sins of *many*. But from the fourth song's perspective, the Servant—for all his personal characteristics—had to maintain his vital link with the collectivity of Israel. As H. H. Rowley concludes, we must allow for both possibilities within the fourth song: there is a pendulum movement based on some notion of a "corporate personality."[55]

We cannot agree with Delitzsch and Noth and think of a simple linear progression that begins with the Servant as Israel (chap. 42), moves to the faithful remnant (chap. 49), then to the prophet (chap. 50), and concludes with a future person (chap. 53).[56] Rowley shows how the New Testament also manifests this "pendulum movement," first condensing the idea of the Servant by applying it to Jesus, and then expanding it to the doctrine of the church (Phil. 3:10; Rom. 8:17; Col. 1:24; Gal. 2:20).[57]

In the fourth song the Servant is first viewed alone in his exaltation (52:13), but at the end he is clearly and fully identified with his people as he shares the spoils of victory with them (53:12ab; cf. Luke 11:22; Rev. 2:7, 11, 17, 26–28; 3:6, 12, 21). Thus even at its most extreme, Judaism's insistence on a collective interpretation can keep us from interpreting the song in exclusively individualistic terms.

Similarly, liberation theologies warn against the dichotomies and individualistic extremes within the church. They remind us that the Servant of the fourth song came to free us from our highly competitive individualism (53:6), not to strengthen such prejudices. They also remind us that the revelation of the fourth song (a revelation fulfilled but never eclipsed, even in the New Testament) was not given to the church, but to a prophet of Israel—and for a time when the nation would have to pass through the deep waters of exile. A church that has, since Constantine, been too closely identified with the rich and the powerful and not with the sufferings of the poor must never make light of what the synagogue says about the fourth song in relation to the bitter experience of national oppression.

Oppression and Revolution

As we have seen, much of the Servant's suffering in the fourth song is put in terms of a sickness, leprosy in particular. But there is another pole to this complex of suffering—namely, oppression. The psalms show us how frequently persecution followed sickness when enemies took advantage of the situation by making false accusations. But it is difficult to understand what happens to the Servant in the fourth song, inasmuch as a leper was an unclean person, ostracized from the community. Nevertheless here the Servant appears to submit himself to a legal trial resulting in his execution (53:7, 8). However, another verse suggests he died from his sickness at the hands of Yahweh (53:10). Because of this, Westermann insists that we cannot understand this language of suffering literally, whether the suffering be due to sickness or oppression.[58]

What is certain, however, is that the song describes the Servant as the object of widely varied oppression:

> scourged by God and humiliatingly oppressed *('anah)* [53:4d] . . .
> oppressively crushed *(daka')* for our iniquity [5b] . . .
> beaten and driven like an animal *(nagas)* and humiliatingly
>   oppressed *('anah)* [7a] . . .
> by judicial oppression *('otser)* and judgment he was taken away [8a] . . .
> yet it pleased Yahweh to oppress *(daka',* crush) him with sickness [10a].

The song thus uses 4 different Hebrew roots 6 times, making oppression a basic category of its theology. In 7a and 8a it appears that the Servant suffers torture and oppression in a legal, juridical process.But in 4d, 5b, and 10a Yahweh wills the oppression and uses sickness. Concerning the sickness, we hear that the Servant identified with *the people*: the sicknesses were theirs in the first place (4ab). But the text does not say anything about the people's suffering oppression; it was a torment that the Servant alone bore. The indifference of his fellow citizens (8b) possibly shows that he suffered this oppression at the hands of a foreign power (7a and 8a).

Once we properly understand the fourth song's emphasis on how the Servant is oppressed, we can appreciate the repeated announcements of a successful revolution that liberates this poor-oppressed servant and exalts him and his followers. God declares:

> Behold, my Servant shall prosper,
> he shall be high and lifted up,
> and greatly exalted [52:13].

The gentiles are frightened (52:14a) and the kings, instead of accusing him, must keep quiet (52:15b); he carries out Yahweh's just plans (53:10d); he shares the spoils of revolution with his faithful followers (53:12a, b). All this builds up to show how closely the Servant resembles Moses: the exodus story repeatedly stressed that the Israelites had despoiled their Egyptian oppressors when they left the country (Exod. 3:21, 22; 11:2, 3; 12:35, 36). Gustaf Aulen's interpretation of the cross in terms of Christ's triumph may find support in this passage, but such meaning *results* from penal substitution and does *not* supplant it.[59] In this way we can see that the fourth song introduces a kind of theology of oppression similiar to the Magnificat of Mary. God tells us that:

> He has brought down rulers from their thrones
> but has lifted up the humble. . . .
> He has helped his servant Israel,
> remembering to be merciful [Luke 1:52, 54; cf. 1 Sam. 2:1–10].

Poverty and Prosperity

The fourth song is radical in its view of wealth and poverty. We hear no more of the deuteronomic theology that viewed riches as a sign of obedience. On the contrary, the fourth song identifies the rich with the wicked—a common enough perspective among a people suffering under foreign oppression (Prov. 11:28; Mic. 6:12):

> And they made his grave with the wicked *(reshaim')*
> and with a rich man *('ashir)* in his death [Isa. 53:9ab].

Thus originally the rich in the song were understood to be the wicked, taking the verse poetically as synonymous parallelism. The LXX and the Targum followed the same path, even strengthening the identification of the wicked with the rich.[60]

However, the MT also permits us to interpret the verse as antithetic parallelism:

> They gave him *(natan)* his grave among the wicked,
> but *(w)* his tomb was with a rich man,
> because *('al)* he commited no violence
> and there was no deceit in his mouth.

Matthew uses this second possible interpretation as evidence of the fulfilled prophecy of Jesus' burial in the tomb of Joseph of Arimathea (Matt. 27:57). Taken in this way, the rich man is good and the Servant's exaltation begins when he is buried with a rich man instead of with the wicked. The Dead Sea Scrolls support Matthew's reading against that of the MT when they refer to the *tomb* of the rich man, not to his death.[61]

Although such an interpretation is possible, it seems forced or playful. The Hebrew of this verse is best understood as identifying the rich with the wicked. Surely they are the powerful oppressors (53:8a) who executed the innocent Servant (9a). But if verses 8 and 9 speak of the world as it is, God announces a totally different situation in the song's introduction and conclusion. The song begins by declaring a radical change that will result in the oppressed Servant's "prosperity" (52:12ab). Implicit in all this is a total economic revolution that will deprive the wicked rich and enrich the oppressed poor. The Servant is a new Moses who despoils those who oppress his people (Exod. 12:35-36).

Multi-Faceted Salvation

When we look closely at the fourth song in order to grasp its concept of liberation, we see again the pendulum movement between the depiction of the Servant as an individual and as a representative of a group. It is often difficult to be sure whether it is the group or the individual referred to when the various dimensions of salvation are described in the text.

1) As we have noted, evangelical tradition has properly focused both on rebellion and guilt as the basic problem dealt with in the song, and on the Servant's suffering our condemnation and punishment as the solution. This way he achieved the "justification" of the guilty parties (53:11cd). This interpretation is often abused to create a dichotomy by isolating this central element from its context that speaks of multi-faceted liberation.

2) Pentecostal and charismatic theologies offer a needed corrective to this traditional emphasis by taking literally everything that the fourth song (and Matt. 8:17) says about sickness when it affirms that "we are cured" (53:5d) by the Servant's sufferings. These theologies take a step in the direction of a total liberation, but do not follow the new path far enough.

3) The song also emphasizes the Servant's humiliation and oppression. Thus, God's words at the beginning and end assure us of the Servant's success and eventual exaltation (52:13; 53:10, 12), *which will liberate his people from oppression and humiliation.*

4) The song refers harshly to the wickedness of the rich, but God proclaims at the beginning and end the exalted Servant's prosperity, in which he will share spoils from the rich with his faithful followers. Thus *liberation from poverty* is one dimension of the salvation the Servant achieves.

5) The song describes the alienation that the Servant suffered (53:3d) and the class struggle expressed in the judicial oppression that resulted in his death (53:7a, 8a), but also affirms that the Servant brought *shalom* ("prosperity, health, peace") to his people (53:5c).

6) Throughout the song, we see the Servant in terrible situations of isolation and loneliness (53:3cd, 4cd, 8b), but at last he appears in relationships of solidarity and fellowship *(koinonía)* with a multitude of his followers (53:12ab).

7) Because of his isolation, sickness, and fatal oppression, the Servant is

threatened with sterility. But the song concludes that "he will see his offspring" (53:10d), a theme exuberantly developed in the following chapter (54:1-8, 11-13) as *liberation from barrenness.*

8) Throughout the song the Servant's death frequently is indicated (53:8acd, 9ab, 10b, 12c). Many believe that his resurrection is also suggested, partly because of New Testament influence, partly because of pagan myths of gods who were resurrected.[62] Dahood insists that the text speaks rather of eternal life in paradise and not necessarily of resurrection. The key text literally says: "he shall see light and be satisfied" (53:11ab). The MT does not include an object for the verb "will see," as does the LXX, "light" *(fōs)*. One Dead Sea Scroll (IQIs³) supports the LXX reading, and so more recent English versions (NIV, NEB) follow the LXX.

Light in Isaiah is a favorite symbol for liberation from oppression (Assyrian oppression, 9:2; Babylonian, 42:6; 49:6), particularly in the Servant Songs. It also represents healing (42:16; 58:8). When we compare the same expression ("to see light") with Psalm 36:8, 9, we can see that it may also describe the happiness of eternal life in terms of a messianic banquet.[63] Hence, at the very least the song speaks of *liberation from oppression and death* in the same way as does Luke 1:77-79 and 23:43 ("today you will be with me in paradise"). But does it also suggest resurrection? The verbs in 52:13 may be understood this way, although they normally have a more general meaning. Possibly the Servant's exaltation (52:13) suggests that even his body is involved in his rehabilitation, especially when we compare this with the gentiles' and their kings' reaction in 52:14, 15. The expression "he will see his offspring, he shall prolong *('arac)* his days" (53:10d) strongly suggests that earthly life will continue. This is more consistent with the Old Testament hope of celebrating a military victory (53:12ab) as something that will occur on earth. Certainly the Servant's experience includes liberation from oppression and death: light after the darkness of prison and the grave, whether that be in a heavenly paradise, on earth with a resurrected body, or both.

9) Although nothing in the fourth song explicitly suggests a liberation from exile and a return to the land, we cannot ignore the immediate context: the author or editor, guided by the Holy Spirit, placed the fourth song *immediately* after the previous chapters had climaxed with the call to leave Babylon and return to Zion (52:7-12). Liberation from sin and its guilt occurs precisely in a context that proclaims *liberation from the oppression of the exile*—that is, the new exodus that results in a return to the land. The Servant's death is likened to the death of the Passover lamb (Exod. 12) as the necessary sacrifice that not only liberates from sin and guilt, but also from Babylonian oppression. Christians who insist on verbal inspiration should be the first to recognize that such inspiration also implies a "structural" inspiration and thus should accept the theological implications of the structure of a prophetic book.

10) Furthermore the fourth song's context also speaks of an *ecological liberation that transforms nature.* The Babylonian invaders had left the Holy

Land in ruins: vegetation was destroyed and continuous droughts resulted. Again and again Isaiah 40–55 speaks in exalted terms of the regeneration of the earth, the ecological redemption that will accompany the people's return to its land. The book ends by proclaiming the new earth—Eden restored (55:10–13; cf. 35:1, 2, 6b–7; 41:17–20; 43:18–21; 49:8–13, 19; also 65:17–25). As Moltmann insists:

> One can never achieve any liberation from economic poverty, political oppression and human alienation without making peace with nature and liberating her from inhuman exploitation.[64]

Situating the fourth song in its context, the salvation proclaimed there is an integral, multi-faceted liberation that embraces justification from the guilt of sin; healing of sicknesses; liberation from oppression; prosperity instead of poverty; peace instead of class struggle; fellowship and *koinonia* instead of loneliness and scorn; demographic growth instead of barrenness and the extermination of the nation; eternal life in paradise and (possibly) resurrection of the body instead of death; the return to the land instead of exile and oppression; and a new, fertile land instead of an ecological wasteland.

The Servant's Praxis

We have already examined the basic elements in the role developed by the Servant: his incarnational identification with his people in their exile and oppression, and his vicarious suffering of the punishment and condemnation of sin. In this section I wish to point out, however briefly, other footprints in the Servant's road.

Scorn, Loneliness. At the very time the Servant does most to redeem others, he experiences their cruel contempt—alienation and lack of understanding instead of gratitude: "He was despised *(bzh)* and rejected by men . . . he was despised *(bzh)* and we esteemed him not" (Isa. 53:3ad). As happened to Job, his compatriots do not understand his sufferings (Isa. 53:4cd). He ends up isolated, alienated from his people—"as one from whom people hide their faces" (v. 3c), showing their complete indifference to his suffering: "as for his generation, who considered that he was cut off from the land of the living?" (v. 8bc). In this way the Servant is the complete opposite of charismatic political leaders who attract followers by reason of their powerful personality.

Silence. When we think we are misunderstood, we try to improve the situation by a public relations campaign. If we are oppressed, we organize demonstrations that call attention to our lot. If we are punished unjustly for crimes committed by others, we clamor for vindication. The Servant acted otherwise: "he did not open his mouth . . . like a sheep before its shearers is dumb, so he opened not his mouth" (Isa. 53:7). He did not merely keep a low profile in public life (cf.42:2); in the face of his people's misunderstanding and indifference and in the face of foreign oppression, he maintains total silence.

Of course there are times to shout out the good news (40:9) and to trumpet against sin (58:1), but that was clearly *not* the time (Eccles. 3:7). Because the Servant had already expressed himself (Isa. 50:4, 10) and his hearers had hardened their hearts, it was not meaningful to keep talking: it was time to suffer in silence.

Nonviolence. The Bible establishes a dialectic when it comes to violence. The prophets boldly preach against injustice and oppression. When the gospel sallies forth with its revolutionary implications, wars naturally follow (the white horse of Rev. 6:1–4). We must admit that at least *indirectly* the gospel may foster some kind of violence against an unjust status quo maintained by oppression. But make no mistake: the Servant does not follow the path of violence. Faced with the most unjust oppression, "he committed no violence *(ḥamas)*" (53:9c).

Biblically, we must distinguish between violence and legitimate force. Governments claim the right to use legitimate force, even to put to death (Rom. 13), but that is not what the Bible terms "violence." Isaiah became so enthusiastic about Cyrus (whose military victories made Israel's liberation from Babylon possible) that he refers to him as Yahweh's "anointed messiah" (Isa. 41:2, 3; 44:28–45:6; 48:14, 15). In reference to guerrilla warfare, such as the Maccabean conflicts, the Bible considers them of "little help" (Dan. 11:34), even though such conflicts may be highly successful in human terms. Jesus used destructive force to cleanse the temple, but he did so only as a Son in his Father's house, where he had the legitimate authority to do so. He did not kill or follow a path of violence in relation to his people's struggles. He preferred to suffer martyrdom rather than do violence. Therefore, God exalted him (52:13) and gave him the victory (53:12).

(See also "Excursus: Nonviolent Force and Institutionalized Violence," chap. 6, below.)

The Pure Truth. It is one thing not to lie; but it is something else to avoid any kind of deceit, especially if there is chance of encountering the police or some force that could endanger your life. The Servant chose a lofty course: "neither was there deceit *(mirmah)* in his mouth" (53:9d). He never tried to justify white lies or dirty tricks by claiming that the end justifies the means. He never took recourse in deceit or demagogy even in order to liberate the poor and oppressed. At the end of his life, he suffered personal oppression in silence. But there had been a time when he spoke—and then it was the pure truth.

Intercession. Some exegetes deny that the Servant's praxis in the fourth song involves prayer. Westermann points out that the verb *pg'* in 53:12f has a much broader range of meanings.[65] The lexicons offer such definitions as "encounter, meet, fall in with, put pressure on someone, urge strongly on someone, fall upon, attack" (Hol., p. 288). The same verb occurs in Isaiah 53:6 in the hiphil form, which the NEB translates: "but the Lord *laid upon* him the guilt of us all." So there is no doubt that the verb has a broader range of meaning than "intercede." Westermann wishes to understand its use in 53:12f as synonymous with 53:12e ("he bore the sin of many"). He says that the following verb simply means that the Servant intervened for the rebels: "He took their place and suffered their punishment in their stead."[66]

But there is no doubt that the verb *pg'* can include the idea of intercession (Jer. 7:16). For this reason Young's conclusion is preferable: in 53:12f, "the intercession refers not merely to prayer, but includes the bearing of sin."[67] In this way the Servant's *entire* priestly work finds expression in the verb (cf. Rom. 8:34; Heb. 9:24; 1 John 2:21; also, the Servant's exaltation at the beginning of the song with the goal of "sprinkling" the nations, 52:13-15). Thus the Song concludes not with a decontextualized prayer, something unrelated to life's totality, but with an intercession based on a sacrificial life. Since the intercession is directed to Yahweh, the song's conclusion reminds us that humanity's fundamental problem is not oppression or captivity, but guilt before a righteous God.

Exaltation: Power and Effectiveness. One of the primary considerations in the fourth song is *how* Yahweh shows his power. In the context the prophet repeatedly uses the image of the "arm" to point to Yahweh's activity (Isa. 49:10; 51:5, 9; 52:10). We may say that Cyrus acted as Yahweh's "left hand" to liberate Israel from Babylonian oppression. Cyrus—not the Servant—is called Yahweh's "anointed" (*m^eshiho;* 45:1). Still, the captivity is not the most difficult problem. God can easily liberate the people from captivity (49:24-26). But who can free the people from the guilt of sin in the face of a God who is perfectly holy and just (Isa. 6)? Here a "deeper magic" is needed (C. S. Lewis). Few understand or properly appreciate the power that justifies the guilty sinner. Thus the prophet is moved to reflect: "And to whom has the arm of the Lord been revealed?" (53:1b). In a certain sense this question is the theme of the fourth song. Paul uses this to articulate his theology of the cross when he sees that "the weakness of God is stronger than men" (1 Cor. 1:25) and that "God chose what is weak in the world to shame the strong" (1 Cor. 1:27).

As Hugo Assmann points out, according to Paul the power of Christ "is not mere words." When we "reject the drivel that says that Christ's power cannot be defined . . . [we can precisely] determine 'where' Christ's power acts in the conflicts of human history."[68] Assmann astutely observes:

> Those mournful Christs in Latin America, whose central image is only the cross, are Christs who express the powerlessness that the oppressed have internalized. . . . On the other hand, those rare triumphant Christs in Latin America, those who are seated on thrones, wearing crowns like the kings of Spain, those are not "other," different Christs. . . . They are the other face of the same Christs, the face that oppressors were used to seeing.
>
> So there is no way to separate the cross from the resurrection without falling prey to alienating Christs. The Christs of the established power (who do not need to fight, because they rule) and the Christs of the

established powerlessness (who cannot fight, because they are oppressed) are two faces of oppressive christologies.[69]

What is Required of the People: Commitment

Obviously the author of the fourth song hoped that many would benefit from the Servant's sacrifice. But is that something that automatically happens without the people's fulfilling certain conditions? The song does not treat this theme systematically, but we do find specific guidelines in both the song itself and its immediate context.

Believe the Good News. When the "we" begin to speak in Isaiah 53, the basic concern is that the hearers believe the *un*believable news soon to be announced: "Who has believed what we have heard?" (53:1a). The next, parallel line suggests that the faith that believes such news would depend on a special divine revelation in order to emphasize God's presence and power where humans would least expect it (cf. Matt.16:17). Thus one basic concern in the fourth song is the need to trust the report about the Servant: his origin, oppression, death, and exaltation.

Confession. This condition is the most carefully elaborated in the fourth song and consists of two parts: *confession* of sin and *profession* of trust that the Servant did all that was needed to solve the problem of our rebellion and guilt before God. The confession of sin is collective, and admits no exceptions:

> All we like sheep have gone astray:
> we have turned every one to his own way [53:6].

The second element of this confession highlights a radical change from an attitude of disgust toward the Servant (53:3) to one that recognizes that he has done everything necessary to justify us and reconcile us with God:

> Yet on himself he bore our sufferings,
> our torments he endured . . .
> but he was pierced for our transgressions,
> tortured for our iniquities . . .
> but the Lord laid upon him
> the guilt of us all [53:4–7, NEB].

Conversion. One kind of conversion stands out in the fourth song and highlights the radical change in attitude to the Servant. That we not overlook the real point of the song, the prophet concludes chapters 40–55 with a bold call to repentance. This rings out in a genuinely evangelistic invitation:

> Come, all who are thirsty, come, fetch water;
> come, you who have no food, buy corn and eat;
> come and buy, not for money, not for a price
> [MT adds: "wine and milk"; 55:1, NEB].

Seek the Lord while he may be found;
call on him while he is near.
Let the wicked forsake his way
and the evil man his thoughts.
Let him turn to the Lord, and he will
have mercy on him,
and to our God, for he will freely pardon [55:7–8, NIV].

Neither Billy Graham nor Luis Palau could have sounded a clearer, more stirring call to authentic repentance.

Participation in Historical Undertakings. But let us not identify the prophet's call to repentance with similar efforts that certain evangelists of a fundamentalist stripe carry out today. Above all else, Isaiah emphasizes that God expects participation in a particular historical undertaking—namely, the new exodus, from Babylonian oppression, and the return to Palestine. Thus the "comfort" (chap. 40–52) reaches its goal in the urgent command in 52:11: "Away from Babylon; come out, come out!" (NEB). The repetition of the verbs emphasizes how pressing the order is. God is not merely a transcendent and holy God (Isa. 6); he is a God profoundly involved in human history. To "seek" him is, therefore, to do more than cry and pray for pardon; it is also to cooperate with him in his acts of liberation and justice within the march of history. Not to move along with him in paths of liberation is to wander about like unintelligent sheep.We must understand the call to repent and seek God in Isaiah 55 within the context of the foregoing chapters, especially in the final order to escape from captivity and return to the promised land (52:11, 12). By not cooperating with God in his historical undertaking of liberation, one falls into nothing less than rebellion and unbelief (cf. Num. 13–14).

In Christian thought it is common to consider such divine "historical undertakings" within the theological category of "social ethics." But Isaiah opens up a new perspective. Within the canonical ordering of the books' chapters, this collaboration with God in his historical march (52:11, 12) *precedes* the passage in which the significance of the Servant's death is revealed. Undoubtedly many Israelites responded to God in that fundamental collaboration without fathoming the depths reached in the message of the fourth song. Hence we should understand this collaboration in historical undertakings as something that may come *before* the full response to the good news as a way we manifest our common humanity. If we do not obey the command on this basic level (as thousands of unbelievers already do), how can we ever hope to respond to God on the deeper level of understanding the Servant and sharing in his sufferings (Phil. 3:10; Col. 1:24)?[70]

CONCLUSIONS

We may identify three streams within Latin American theology that provide distinct but essential perspectives for the interpretation *(relectura)* of Isaiah 52:13–53:12.

Historical Catholic and Protestant traditions help us focus on humanity's central problem (i.e., rebellion and guilt in relation to a just and holy God) and explain the Servant's work in the biblical terms of penal substitution. They do not try to pander to modern prejudices, though many today prefer not to think either of a just God or of the need for a propitiatory sacrifice for their sin.

The Pentecostal perspective forces us to take seriously the Bible's description of the Servant's sickness and the Bible's call to proclaim and practice healing of the sick as an essential element of the gospel and Christian praxis.

Judaism and various liberation theologies teach us to recognize the fourth song's original historical context (i.e., liberation from injustice, oppression, and exile); the Servant's identification with his people Israel; the rich vocabulary of "oppression" in which the Servant's sufferings are made concrete; salvation as total liberation; and repentance as a turning to the God of the Bible—which involves collaboration with him in his historical march forward to liberation.

We dare not eliminate any of these three perspectives if we want to discover in the fourth song all that God would say to us. As Peter points out, the message of the cross has three unmistakable and inseparable dimensions:

> He himself bore our sins in his body on the tree [evangelical],
> that we might die to sin and live to justice [liberational].
> By his wounds you have been healed [pentecostal; 1 Pet. 2:24].

In Isaiah 53, as elsewhere in Scripture, these three dimensions—the evangelical, the pentecostal, and the Latin American liberationist—illuminate and mutually strengthen each other—and a cord of three strands is not quickly broken (Eccles.4:12).

Chapter 6

Jubilee and Our
Central American Colonies

ISAIAH 58 AND THE JUBILEE YEAR

"Shout it aloud, do not hold back. Raise your voice like a trumpet. Declare to my people their rebellion and to the house of Jacob their sins.

"For day after day they seek me out; they seem eager to know my ways, as if they were a nation that does what is right and has not forsaken the commands of its God. They ask me for just decisions and seem eager for God to come near them.

" 'Why have we fasted,' they say, 'and you have not seen it? Why have we humbled ourselves, and you have not noticed?' Yet on the day of your fasting, you do as you please and exploit all your workers.

"Your fasting ends in quarreling and strife, and in striking each other with wicked fists. You cannot fast as you do today and expect your voice to be heard on high.

"Is this the kind of fast I have chosen, only a day for a man to humble himself? Is it only for bowing one's head like a reed and for lying on sackcloth and ashes? Is that what you call a fast, a day acceptable to the Lord?

"Is not this the kind of fasting I have chosen: to loose the chains of injustice and untie the cords of the yoke, *to set the oppressed free* and break every yoke?

"Is it not to share your food with the hungry and to provide the poor wanderer with shelter—when you see the naked, to clothe him, and not to turn away from your own flesh and blood?

"Then your light will break forth like the dawn, and your healing will quickly appear; then your righteousness will go before you, and the glory of the Lord will be your rear guard.

"Then you will call, and the Lord will answer; you will cry for help, and he will say: Here am I. If you do away with the yoke of oppression, with the pointing finger and malicious talk,

"and if you spend yourselves on behalf of the hungry and satisfy the needs of the oppressed, then your light will rise in the darkness, and your night will become like the noonday.

"The Lord will guide you always; he will satisfy your needs in a sun-scorched land and will strengthen your frame. You will be like a well-watered garden, like a spring whose waters never fail.

"Your people will rebuild the ancient ruins and will raise up the age-old foundations; you will be called Repairer of Broken Walls, Restorer of Streets with Dwellings.

"If you keep your feet from breaking the Sabbath and from doing as you please on my holy day, if you call the Sabbath a delight and the Lord's holy day honorable, and if you honor it by not going your own way and not doing as you please or speaking idle words,

"then you will find your joy in the Lord, and I will cause you to ride on the heights of the land and to feast on the inheritance of your father Jacob." The mouth of the Lord has spoken [Isa. 58:1–14, NIV; italics added].

The Spirit of the Lord is on me, because he has anointed me to preach good news to the poor. He has sent me to proclaim freedom for the prisoners and recovery of sight for the blind, *to release the oppressed*, to proclaim the year of the Lord's favor [Luke 4:18–19; italics added].

The insertion of the phrase from Isaiah 58:6 (literally, "to send the oppressed away liberated") in the midst of Jesus' citation of Isaiah 61:1–2 in the synagogue at Nazareth (Luke 4:18–19) appears never to have been adequately explained. R.T. France concludes that "it does not affect the sense,"[1] a conclusion I intend to challenge. I. Howard Marshall goes so far as to say "The insertion adds nothing to the sense, and it is hard to see why it was made."[2] With a kind of counsel of despair, he concludes: "The conflation of two prophetic passages can hardly have taken place in a synagogue reading, and it is probably due to Christian exegetical activity."[3] Surprisingly, so obvious a problem in a text so foundational to Jesus' understanding of his mission until recently received sparse attention in the standard commentaries and scholarly literature.[4]

The hypothesis I propose to defend here is that the insertion of Isaiah 58:6 in Isaiah 61:1–2 is best explained by recognizing that both of them reflect the teaching of Leviticus 25 concerning the Year of Jubilee, and that the originality and boldness exemplified in relating the two texts is best accounted for as reflecting Jesus' own exegetical insight and passion for *liberation* (not just "forgiveness," as Marshall suggests).[5]

That Isaiah 61:1–2 refers to the Year of Jubilee is so widely recognized as to need no defense.[6] Strangely, the relation between Isaiah 58 and the Jubilee is only beginning to be noticed.[7] The following evidence points clearly in that direction.

1) Structurally, Isaiah 58:1–12 occurs in a section purposefully framed as sabbatarian teaching. As Westermann, commenting on Isaiah 58:13–14, puts it: "Since a new section begins in chapter 59, one may surmise that the two admonitions concerning the Sabbath, 56:1 f. and 58:13 f., were deliberately designed as a framework for the section composed of chapters 56–58."[8] The Jubilee, as a Sabbath year, also occurs in a sabbatarian context (Lev. 23:1–3; 25:1–7). The conclusion of the Jubilee teaching even includes an exhortation to Sabbath keeping (Lev. 26:2) that is remarkably similar to Isaiah 58:13–14.

2) The basic question and theme of Isaiah 58 is what constitutes proper fasting (vv. 3–6). Although four other fasts began to be observed in the postexilic period (Zech. 7:3; 8:18), the only fast *commanded* in the law is that of the Day of Atonement (Lev. 26:29–31). The Year of Jubilee began precisely on that day (Lev. 25:9), the day of fasting *par excellence*. Westermann points out the problem that came to be associated with the additional fasts and concludes that Isaiah 58:12 "contributed toward their being given up."[9] Because the fast of the Day of Atonement, prescribed by the law, could scarcely be abandoned, we may say that Isaiah 58:1–12 proposes the proper observance of the one true fast, including the Jubilee provisions for the poor, as opposed to the multiplication of purely religious rites devoid of ethical content (cf. Zech. 7:3–7, 8–10).

The one true fast is twice designated as the fast that Yahweh "chooses" *(bahar),* 58:5, 6. It includes the Jubilee provisions for socio-economic revolution in contrast to the later tendency to multiply religious rites devoid of ethical content. P. Volz argues: "Everything suggests that the prophetic leader was speaking in public; perhaps in the synagogue at an assembly for fasting."[10]

3) Isaiah 58 begins with the divine exhortation to the prophet:

> Cry with all your might, spare not,
> lift up your voice like a trumpet *(shophar).* [58:1ab]

The inauguration of the Year of Jubilee was to be announced with mighty blasts from the trumpet *(shophar)* to be heard throughout all the land (Lev. 25:9). The word "jubilee" itself translates a rarer word for what was evidently a special kind of trumpet *(yobel)*. With trumpetlike voice the prophet is called upon to

> declare to my people their transgression
> and to the house of Jacob their sins [58:1cd].

Such a declaration would be particularly appropriate for the Day of Atonement, when the Jubilee began.[11] Because Jacob was infamous for having coveted and stolen his brother's birthright and blessing, and thereby (temporarily) lost all in exile from his father's house (Gen. 27–35), the prophet refers to Israel's sin (neglect of justice for the poor, coveting and seizing of their lands) by the patriarch's name.

4) Isaiah 58:2 refers to an ordinance *(mishpat)* of God that has been forsaken, resulting in gross injustice and oppression. The Jubilee law, Israel's surest guarantee of a just social order, was also one of the most neglected. Although recent scholarship challenges older tendencies to write off the Jubilee as an absurdly idealistic priestly notion,[12] undoubtedly it is the provision of the Torah that best qualifies for the description of a forsaken ordinance.

5) Isaiah 58:5 refers to the fast day (the Day of Atonement) as an "acceptable day" *(yom ratson)*, whereas Isaiah 61:2 speaks of an "acceptable *year*" *(shenath ratson)*. The latter unquestionably refers to the Year of Jubilee (cf. the proclamation of liberty to captives, 61:1). That is to say, the "acceptable *year*" (Jubilee, Isa. 61:3) is to be inaugurated by the "acceptable *day*" (Isa. 58:5), the fast day of Atonement.

6) As Jesus discerned (perhaps during his 40-day fast in the wilderness), Isaiah 58:6 is a clear reference to the basic provision of the Jubilee (general emancipation of slaves to return to their patrimonies), inaugurated by the fast day of Atonement:

> Is not this the fast that I choose,
> to loose the fetters of injustice
> to untie the thongs of the yoke bar
> and to send the oppressed away liberated
> —that you smash every yoke bar?

The reference to the Jubilee is seen most clearly in the provision to send away (back to their patrimony and clan) emancipated slaves. However, as Westermann points out, liberation is the single theme of each of the last four lines of the verse (cf. the following verse, where four lines describe four distinct acts).[13] The "fetters of injustice" refer to slaves unjustly maintained, contrary to the Torah, which provided for their freedom at the end of six years of service.[14]

Although linguistically the action of sending slaves away liberated need not refer to the Jubilee liberation, it is quite appropriate as a description of that event. Moreover, all alternative candidates for the "neglected ordinance" are ruled out by various factors:

   (a) Exodus 21:1-6 and Deuteronomy 15:12-18 do not describe a general emancipation: according to these ordinances, slaves were to be freed when their six years of service were completed.
   (b) Deuteronomy 15:1-11 refers to the termination or suspension of debts but says nothing about freeing of slaves.
   (c) Leviticus 25:1-7 provides that the land must lie fallow every Sabbath year but says nothing about freeing of slaves.

Thus only the Jubilee provisions of Leviticus 25:8-55 unite the various factors referred to in Isaiah 58.[15]

Westermann, having pointed out the fourfold stress in Isaiah 58:6 on setting slaves free, concludes: "release from any sort of bondage is given pride of place."[16] This is explained as historically grounded in the people's recent experience: "a direct repercussion of what the entire nation had had experience of, bondage in the exile."[17] The Jubilee laws conclude with a similar emphasis:

> For to me the people of Israel are servants, they are my servants whom I brought forth out of the land of Egypt: I am the Lord your God [Lev. 25:55].

7) Although the divinely ordained fast is to be observed particularly by the dynamic socio-political action of liberating enslaved debtors and by the radical economic measure of restoring their properties to them, the needs of some were too urgent to await the benefits of the drastic socio-political structural changes. Hence, the prophet also says of the divinely ordained fast:

> Does it not mean sharing your bread with the hungry
> and bringing the homeless poor into your house,
> when you see someone naked, to cover him
> and not to withdraw yourself from your own flesh?
> [Isa. 57:8; cf. v.10].

Thus again the fast ordained by Yahweh follows the pattern of the Jubilee provisions, where Israel is commanded to take the homeless poor into its own house (Lev. 25:35c, 36c) and to provide them food without charge (25:35, 37b). The command "not to withdraw yourself from your own flesh *(basar)*" may reflect the stress on the "brother" in the redemption regulations in the latter half of Leviticus 25 (vv. 25, 35-37, 47). There the passage extends the term to include the stranger and sojourner.[18]

The programmatic nature of Isaiah 58 in Jesus' thinking is evidenced by the fact that he not only boldly inserts the phrase from 58:6 in his *inaugural* sermon at Nazareth, but also, according to Matthew's Gospel, *concludes* his teaching with a parable on the final judgment (the separation of the sheep and goats) that elaborates Isaiah 58:7.[19]

8) One of the basic provisions of the Year of Jubilee is the canceling of all debts (Lev. 25:10, 35–55; cf. Deut. 15:1–11). Commentators have been perplexed by the assertion in Isaiah 58:4a:

> Your fasting leads only to wrangling and strife
> and dealing vicious blows with the fist [NEB].

It seems utterly inadequate to account for such violent reactions by saying "the fasters become irritable and upset."[20] It is surely preferable to relate the violence expressed in 4a to the situation described in 3b in the translation suggested by L. Koehler and W. Kessler:[21]

> Behold, in the day of your fast you pursue your own business and dun your debtors.[22]

Anyone who knows something of the brutal methods of debt collecting used against the poor even in contemporary U.S.A., particularly by loan sharks, will not be surprised that violence was associated with attempts to dun the poor in Israel. Such actions stand in brazen contrast with the canceling of debts and freeing of slaves prescribed by divine law as part of the true fast in Leviticus 25 and Isaiah 58.

9) In Isaiah 58:9b we have a further clue to the Jubilee context of the prophet's sermon:

> If you get rid of the yoke bars,
> Stop pointing the accusing finger and laying false charges,
> If you feed the hungry from your own plenty
> And satisfy the needs of the oppressed. . . .

The pointing of the finger is thus best understood as reflecting accusation and "false charges" (NEB), not as ridicule.[23] Undoubtedly the account of Jezebel's intrigue to seize Naboth's vineyard for King Ahab represents an extreme case. But one can well imagine countless similar intrigues and petty charges rationalized into excuses for continued oppression of the poor. The proclamation of the Jubilee demanded that Israelite landholders restore the property rights of enslaved debtors. Undoubtedly many at such a time were tempted to rationalize and institutionalize their positions of privilege with trumped up charges and by circulating false rumors about the immorality and laziness of the poor and their incapacity to manage their own affairs. In the face of such rationalizations of privilege, the prophet calls upon the rich and powerful to fulfill their jubilee obligations to the letter, eliminating the yoke bars of slavery and feeding the hungry poor.

10) In his inaugural synagogue sermon at Nazareth, Jesus cites the Jubilee text, Isaiah 61:1–2, making the most explicit Jubilee reference ("to proclaim the acceptable year of the Lord") his conclusion. He breaks the parallelism of the Hebrew poetry, omitting the concluding reference to "the day of vengeance of our God." This, I believe, is done not to negate the reality of divine judgment (as liberals have sometimes argued): elsewhere such a judgment is abundantly affirmed in his teaching. Nor can we say that Jesus merely wants to stress "forgiveness."[24]

Rather Jesus' intention is best understood as placing all possible stress on the programmatic nature of the Jubilee Year for his own ministry of liberation. His intention to emphasize the Jubilee-type liberation, which might be missed by the subtle device of the cutoff point in the Scripture reading, is made inescapably clear by the bold and abrupt insertion of the phrase from Isaiah 58:6 ("to send the captives away liberated"). His intention and exegetical insight is made particularly clear by the choice of the most explicit Jubilee phrase in the verse that most stresses (four synonymous lines) the Jubilee liberation—Isaiah 58:6.[25]

The "sending" clearly refers, then, to the freeing of the slaves and returning their patrimony to them. The climactic promise of Isaiah 58:14c is particularly appropriate to this Jubilee theme. As the NEB renders it: "and your father Jacob's patrimony shall be yours to enjoy." The reference to Jacob is undoubtedly a deliberate allusion to the patriarch's name in 58:1d, forming a kind of inclusion and indicating the unity of the chapter. Far from an unrelated bit of sabbatarian teaching, vv. 13–14, stressing the glories of Sabbath *day* observance, form a fitting conclusion to a chapter proclaiming the importance of Jubilee Sabbath *year* observance. The Sabbath day, as Deuteronomy clearly taught (5:12–15, motive clause) was to be a miniature, weekly, exodus-type liberation, especially for the working class; the Sabbath year of the Jubilee represented the same kind of exodus-liberation writ large. The surest way to enjoy the fruits of ancestral patrimonies, the prophet promises, is not by coveting and seizing (or keeping) the lands of others, but by faithfully observing the liberating provision of the weekly Sabbath and the Jubilee Sabbath year.[26]

I conclude, then, that Isaiah 58 shows abundantly its relationship with the Jubilee teaching of Leviticus 25. This relationship makes it easy to appreciate the aptness of Jesus' insertion of a phrase from Isaiah 58:6 in his citation of Isaiah 61:1–2 in his sermon at Nazareth. By this method he was able to underscore the liberating dimension of his own ministry and his understanding of the kingdom of God as involving the kind of socio-economic revolution envisioned in the Jubilee provision.[27] A Jewish writer points out that the Old Testament's Sabbath year laws are "the most radical social legislation prior to the twentieth century."[28]

The precise textual tradition utilized in Luke 4:18–19 (following neither MT nor LXX exactly) may well reflect "Christian exegetical activity."[29] But the boldness and originality evidenced in the linking of Isaiah 58:6 and 61:1–2 is best explained as rooted in Jesus' own prophetic insight.[30]

JUBILEE AND THE PANAMA CANAL

In a recent article on the Jubilee Year, A. van Selms concludes: "Applied to nations, the principles underlying the jubilee condemn permanent colonialism and unbridled exploitation of the soil to the detriment of its inhabitants."[31]

It would be difficult to find a more succinct description of traditional U.S.A. colonialism in Latin America, epitomized from 1964 to 1977 in the battle over a new treaty for the Panama Canal. Though millions of Americans duly celebrated with much fervor the 1976 bicentennial of their own revolution and liberation, they were not ready for some "yoke-shattering" for those whom the U.S.A. oppresses. More recently, military aid to bolster the position of wealthy landholders in El Salvador repeats the scenario.

Will a cracked Liberty Bell bearing the words of Leviticus 25:10 continue as the most appropriate symbol for a nation that preaches liberty but practices colonialism and oppression? One fears that should Jesus repeat his revolutionary Jubilee-based sermon in almost any of our churches, we would seek to push him over a cliff (undoubtedly accompanied by denunciations of "Marxist violence").

In 1977, when a group of Latin evangelical professionals pointed out the applicability of biblical Jubilee teaching to the Panama Canal question, one prominent North American Evangelical theologian objected vociferously. The application, he argued, is inappropriate because it would be virtually impossible to trace the "real original owners." This objection, however, fails to catch the basic principle and essential spirit of the Jubilee laws, which is to assure just economic relationships and avoid extremes of poverty and wealth.[32] On this basis the eighth-century prophets castigated their contemporaries who "join house to house, who add field to field," callous to the rights and needs of the poor.[33] When the present struggle began in El Salvador, an oligarchy of fourteen families had come to control 90 percent of the land. According to the teaching of Moses and Isaiah, these families had flagrantly broken the command "thou shalt not steal."[34]

The North American theologian's attempt to exempt the U.S.A. from its responsibility to practice liberating justice in Latin America sounds all too much like the Pharisees' rationalizations unmasked by our Lord:

> How well you set aside the commandment of God in order to maintain your tradition! Moses said, "Honor your father and your mother," and "The man who curses his father or mother must suffer death." But you hold that if a man says to his father or mother, "Anything of mine which might have been used for your benefit is Corban" (meaning, set apart for God), he is no longer permitted to do anything for his father or mother.

Thus by your own tradition, handed down among you, you make God's word null and void. And many other things that you do are just like that [Mark 7:9-13, NEB].

North American Christians have a tradition of capitalism. We need to beware lest our tradition make us deaf to the revolutionary social teaching of Christ and the Scriptures he came to fulfill.[35] If Christians in North America can learn to listen to their Fellow Christians in Latin America, they may discover what it means to preach a gospel that is truly good news to the poor (Luke 4:18-19). If, instead of the biblical gospel, we are concerned rather to provide "rationalizations for the rich," we are in fact preaching "another gospel" (Gal. 1:6-9; 2 Cor.8:9).[36]
(See also Appendix, below.)

EXCURSUS: NONVIOLENT FORCE AND INSTITUTIONALIZED VIOLENCE

The Latin American mass media (press, radio, television) commonly label the activities of guerrillas and others who use arms to overthrow a government "violence." But when governments resort to the same tactics, the media call it "force." Unfortunately even theologians have written much about violence without trying first to check out its meaning in the Bible.

The distinction between "force" and "violence" is denied by some Christian scholars (Jacques Ellul,[37] Giulio Girardi,[38] Paul Tournier[39]), but it is a distinction made by the Bible. Traditionally the churches have distinguished between "legitimate force"—something legal that defends the established order—and "violence"—something illegal that attempts to overthrow the established order. The Bible does not support this distinction.

Violence in the Old Testament

Old Testament Hebrew uses the root *hamas* to express violence. The noun appears 60 times and the verb just 8 times. Although no one appears to have studied these words thoroughly, I offer the following tentative conclusions as a hypothesis from a preliminary study.

1) The Old Testament roundly condemns violence. "The Lord . . . hates with all his soul the lover of violence" (Ps. 11:5). The oppressed Servant does not respond with violence to the institutionalized violence that drags him to his death:

although he had done no violence and there was no deceit in his mouth
[Isa. 53:9b; cf. Prov. 3:31].

2) The Old Testament distinguishes between violence and just or legitimate force, but it is not the traditional distinction that such theologians as Augus-

tine, Aquinas, and Calvin have made. They distinguished between legal force and illegal force—that is, violence. The Old Testament distinguishes between what is just (force) and unjust (violence). Such is the distinction Jacob made when he prophetically condemned Simeon and Levi ("weapons of *violence* are their swords," Gen. 49:5), but he approves of the legitimate and just force that Judah and the coming Messiah will exercise (49:8–10).

3) The violence that the Old Testament condemns in concrete form is the "institutionalized violence" on the part of rich oppressors. The force with which the poor and oppressed defend themselves never merits the Bible's condemnation, nor is it called "violence."

When Moses killed the Egyptian oppressor in order to save the life of the Israelite slave, the Bible does not term his act "violence," nor does it condemn it (Exod. 2:11–15; cf. Acts 7:23–28). Certain Greek manuscripts (chiefly western) even add after Hebrews 11:23: "By faith, Moses, when he was grown up, destroyed the Egyptian when he observed the humiliating oppression of his brethren"! The textual variant shows us how different early Christians viewed Moses' use of force. Especially since the last century some commentators have suggested that God punished Moses with forty years in exile for his use of "violence," though the text in Exodus says nothing of the sort.

The Bible never condemns what the charismatic liberators (anointed by the Spirit) did in the book of Judges in killing their foreign oppressors in order to liberate the oppressed, nor does it call their actions "violent." This distinction also holds for Joshua 1–12—the bloody conquest of the promised land—which the Bible never calls "violence." It is, rather, a "holy war" (or more accurately, "Yahweh's war"), according to biblical theology.

According to Chronicles, David—who fought as a guerrilla leader when Saul was still king—could declare himself "innocent . . . of any violence" (1 Chron. 12:17; cf. Job 16:17).

But we find an abundance of instances in the Old Testament—especially in the prophets—in which it condemns institutionalized violence. Amos charges that rich and powerful oppressors "hoard in their palaces the gains of crime and violence *(ḥamas)*" (3:10).

In Micah God denounces Jerusalem, saying:

> Shall I acquit the man with wicked scales
> and a bag of deceitful weights?
> Your rich men are full of violence *(ḥamas)*
> your inhabitants speak lies [6:11–12].

Similarly in Ezekiel we read:

> You have gone far enough, o princes of Israel! Give up your violence *(ḥamas)* and oppression *(shōd)* and do what is just and right. Stop dispossessing my people, declares the Sovereign Lord [45:9, NIV].

See also Amos 6:3; Jeremiah 6:7; 13:22; 20:8; 22:3; 51:35; Ezekiel 7:23; 8:17; 12:9; 22:16; 45:9; Habakkuk 1:2, 3, 9; Isaiah 59:6; 60:18; Joel 4:19; Obadiah 10; Zephaniah 1:9; 3:4; Jonah 3:8; Malachi 2:6; Micah 3:1-3; Psalm 73:6.

4) God never commits violence. On the contrary, God frees the poor and oppressed from the violence committed by rich oppressors (Ps. 140:2, 5, 12; cf. 18:49). Also, the ideal (messianic) king's basic task is to free the poor from violence committed by oppressors:

> For he shall rescue the needy from their rich oppressors,
> the distressed (*'ani*, oppressed) who have no protector.
> May he have pity on the needy and the poor,
> deliver the poor from death;
> may he redeem them from oppression and violence *(hamas)*
> and may their blood be precious in his eyes [Ps. 72:12-14].

Violence in the New Testament

Except for one text, the New Testament does not refer explicitly to violence. The Greek words sometimes rendered "violence" have a wide range of meaning often better understood as "force" (*bia*, Acts 5:26; 21:35; 27:41; or *biadzomai*, "to deal with forcibly," Matt. 11:12). When Christ cleansed the temple (John 2:13-22; Mark 11:15-19 // Matt. 21:12-17), he used just and legitimate force ("my father's house . . . den of thieves") but not violence.

The closest the New Testament comes to an explicit reference to violence is in Luke 3:14, where John the Baptist forbids soldiers to "extort money by violence"—literally, "shake violently" (Greek: *diaseio*). As in the Old Testament, it is the institutionalized violence of oppressors that is condemned. The "sword" can represent just and legitimate force in the New Testament (Rom. 13:1-7; Luke 22:35-38; 49-51), but we cannot quote such texts as references to violence if nothing points to injustice within the context.

Conclusions

1) We ought to denounce institutionalized violence against the poor, as did the prophets in both the Old and New Testaments.

2) When poor and oppressed persons resort to force or arms in the face of institutionalized violence, we must not condemn them or call for them to submit to oppression. (According to Ellul, only persons of faith can act in a Christian way.)[40] Of course, God, as the Lord of history, can use either violence or force to further his plans (Gen. 45:5-9; Isa. 10:5; etc.).

3) Nevertheless we must not claim to follow a Christian path when we use military arms against an oppressor. The Bible, and especially the New Testament, does not merely reject violence, but it also severely limits the use of

force (Matt. 5; Luke 6; Rom. 12; 1 Pet. 3). Exhortations not to respond with force abound in New Testament praxis. This is but another indication of the persecution and oppression that the New Testament church commonly experienced.

4) The New Testament calls us to militant actions, but in a struggle of *faith* that includes prophetic reproof and "puts on the armor of God" (Eph. 6: 10–20; 2 Cor. 10:3–5).[41] Such militance, which does not put its trust in metal armor, does not contradict, but is in keeping with what God taught throughout the Old Testament (Zech. 4:6; Exod. 14:13, 14; Isa. 30:1–7, 15–17; 31:1–4, etc.). See Daniel 11 for the possible alternatives in the Maccabean era (ca. 165 B.C.):

(a) make compromises with the oppressing empire (Dan. 1);

(b) run away to caves in the desert (Qumran, for example);

(c) guerrilla warfare (the Maccabees), something that is "of little help" (Dan. 11:34);

(d) the way of the cross; martyrdom (Dan. 12:3).

Not without cause has Daniel been called a pacifist tract.[42] The prophet anticipates the kind of praxis set forth in the Sermon on the Mount.[43]

Chapter 7

God So Loved the Third World

Many Latin Americans believe that the message of Jesus Christ serves no meaningful purpose today—that it alienates, domesticates, and oppresses. They see it as the "religion" which Karl Marx called the "opiate of the people." Others affirm along with St. Paul that the biblical gospel is the revolutionary "dynamite" (Rom. 1:16) that will liberate not only humanity but the entire universe (Rom. 8). Who is right?

No one questions the fact that since Constantine's conversion (A.D. 312), church history abounds with instances of misapplied biblical texts and theological teachings used to domesticate and oppress the poor. As a result, rural and urban workers and students throughout the world have been alienated from the church. However, as even Marx and Engels pointed out, things were not always that way: the church sprang up from among oppressed poor and slaves.[1] Many of Marxism's ideals and principles have historical roots in the prophets' denunciations, in Jesus' own teachings, and in the early church's socializing and communal lifestyle.[2]

But today Jesus' teachings suffer much distortion. Those who claim to be his followers fight among themselves, often within the same ecclesiastical organization. For some, to be Jesus' true disciple means to be an "orthodox Christian" who defends the church's traditional theology and politics against any kind of modernistic, leftist incursion: Jesus defends the status quo and its values. For others, to be a true Christian means seeing in Jesus a guerrilla leader such as Che Guevara or Camilo Torres. This type of Christian attacks the status quo to change traditional doctrines, piety, and politics. Others favor a "Protestant Jesus," a church reformer like Martin Luther; or a charismatic leader who heals the sick; or a kind of oriental religious guru. How can such contradictory ideas have cropped up about Jesus and his message?

MISSION AND PURPOSE OF CHRIST

In one key text in the Scriptures Jesus himself clearly explains his mission and purpose. Many Latin American theologians of different ecclesiastical and

109

political persuasions start from this prophetic text in their effort to answer the question: What do true Christian commitment and praxis demand in Latin America today?

We find this text in Luke's Gospel exactly at the beginning of Jesus' ministry (after his baptism and temptation):

> The Spirit of the Lord is on me,
> because he has anointed me
> to preach good news to the poor.
> He has sent me to proclaim liberation to the prisoners
> and recovery of sight for the blind,
> to liberate the oppressed,
> to proclaim the year of the Lord's favor [Luke 4:18–19].

Jesus' Analysis

If we closely examine Jesus' words here, his penetrating analysis of the human situation is soberly realistic and particularly relevant for the Third World.

The Poor. Jesus turned his attention to "the poor," the socio-economic group that made up most of Palestine's population in the first century, as they do today in Latin America. But Jesus did not merely minister *to* them: he cast his lot *with* the poor, as Luke clearly shows when he reports Jesus' virgin birth in chapters 1 and 2. After telling of Jesus' birth to a humble village girl (but one with some revolutionary aspirations, 1:51–54), Luke relates how Jesus submitted himself to John the Baptist's baptism. This John was a kind of socialist prophet who challenged the rich to show sincere repentance by sharing their goods with the poor (3:10, 11). During his temptation after the baptism, Jesus suffered hunger for forty days (4:2).

Thus when Jesus spoke to the poor with "good news," he did so "from below," not "from above." Jesus knew what it was like to suffer as did the poor. Similarly, the Apostle Paul could condense all of his teachings about the incarnation of God's Son in these words:

> For you know the grace of our Lord Jesus Christ, that though he was rich, yet for our sakes he became poor, so that you through his poverty might become rich [2 Cor. 8:9, NIV].

The Captives. The oppressed can withstand the pressure of poverty for a time if they have some hope, if they can see an escape route, a way to change the situation. But in first-century Palestine, as in the Third World today, the vast majority are trapped in their misery, with no way to improve their situation. When we come upon the word "prisoners," we first of all think of criminals or political detainees. But in Jesus' time it was more common to execute criminals than to imprison them for long periods. Most captives, therefore, were in prison not because of crimes but because they were *debtors*.[3] That is, when Jesus turned his attention to the poor *and* prisoners, he was not thinking of two groups, but one: the poor—imprisonment being a result of poverty.

The Oppressed. Next, Jesus describes the poor as "oppressed." Thus he singles out the primary cause of poverty according to the Bible. Between 1960 and 1970, it was common to attribute Third World poverty to "under-development." But the Bible never says that underdevelopment causes poverty. Old Testament Hebrew uses twenty verbal roots that appear more than five hundred times to describe oppression.[4] It clearly teaches that injustice and oppression are the primary causes of poverty.

The Blind. If in this passage "prisoners" and "the oppressed" refer to the poor, we can expect that "the blind" also belong to the same needy grouping, although this is less than obvious to modern readers. But think of the way Luke reports Jesus' approach to Jericho, where he found ". . . a blind man . . . sitting by the roadside *begging*" (18:35). Poverty appears in the context as a related circumstance in six of the seven times Luke mentions blind persons.[5]

Blindness in Luke 4:18 undoubtedly stands for all the sicknesses that the poor suffer; it also points to a miserable dependence and a lack of awareness: "Can a blind man lead a blind man? Will they not both fall into a pit?" (Luke 6:39). That is, it is bad enough to be poor; it is worse to be imprisoned in misery without being able to get out; but worst of all, blindness closes one's eyes to the injustices that produce poverty, oppression, and sickness.

It is clear that the good news (gospel, *god-spel*) that Jesus brings is *for the poor*. He sided with the poor; he spoke to them as one of them. He describes them as prisoners, blind (sick), and oppressed (unjustly forced to remain poor). Of course Jesus also spoke to the rich and invited them to follow him, but his message for them was not generally received as good news (think of the rich young man in Luke 18:18–30).

Jesus' Praxis

In the face of all that the poor suffer (poverty, captivity, oppression, blindness), Jesus dares to offer himself as the divine solution. Just as Jesus' analysis of the situation has four dimensions, so does the solution that he proclaims.

Announcing the Good News (Evangelism). At first glance Jesus' answer hardly seems to solve the problem. The misery and suffering of the poor demand more than words. Will Jesus come to the poor as Moses did, with a long speech, only to discover that they "did not listen to [him], because of their broken spirit and their cruel bondage" (Exod. 6:9)?[6]

In fact, our text stresses the role that Jesus' *words* play: "The Spirit of the Lord . . . has anointed me to preach . . . to proclaim . . . and to proclaim." If we recall that the speaker is the Word, the only begotten Son of the Father who created the universe by his word, we can appreciate better the emphasis on words.[7] The Holy Spirit has *anointed* the speaker—and that makes his words more than mere sounds. They are divine instruments charged with God's own power. Recall how many of Jesus' miracles took place simply by the power of his words!

What precisely is the "good news" that Jesus came to announce to the poor? His words are full of rich associations throughout all of biblical theology. They refer to the coming of God's kingdom (the final, just order) in Jesus' person (Luke 4:43). In its fullest sense the gospel includes the news of Jesus' death and resurrection (1 Cor. 15:1–3). But according to Luke, Jesus wishes here to emphasize that the gospel and the kingdom of God have first of all to do with the poor.

Liberation. Jesus stresses that the good news that he brings is above all a message of liberation and freedom: "He has sent me to proclaim liberation *(áphesis)* to the prisoners . . . to bring liberation *(áphesis)* to the oppressed." All too often the church has fallen into the trap of betraying its true role by legitimizing the oppression that the established order maintains. But Jesus here makes one thing perfectly clear: the authentic gospel is a liberating message; it does not brook oppression and slavery.

The Greek word *áphesis*, translated "freedom" or "liberation," has a wide range of meanings. Luke uses it three times elsewhere in his Gospel where it is usually translated "forgiveness" (liberation from the guilt and punishment of sin). For example, Jesus explains his message in these terms after his resurrection:

> The Christ will suffer and rise from the dead on the third day, and repentance and forgiveness *(áphesis)* of sins will be preached in his name [Luke 24:46–47, NIV].[8]

Some Christians wish to preach a gospel of socio-political liberation to the poor, whereas others want to offer forgiveness of sins to the rich. But Jesus does not offer us the luxury of two gospels, one for the rich and one for the poor. He proclaims *one* liberating-forgiving gospel that is good news for the poor. Of course this good news for the poor could be interpreted as "bad news" for the rich: they must repent of their oppressive practices, identify with the poor, and share their goods. The gospel can be "good news" for the rich only in the sense that it offers them forgiveness and a new life once they have genuinely repented. Luke 4:18–19 forbids us to remove the socio-political dimension from the gospel, *and* Luke 24:46–47 forbids us to limit the gospel to a purely horizontal level by ignoring forgiveness of sins.

Jesus came not only to *preach about* liberation; he says that he came to *liberate* the oppressed. In order to stress this concretely liberating part of his mission, Jesus boldly inserts a phrase from Isaiah 58:6 into his quote from Isaiah 61:1–2. The phrase from Isaiah 58 clearly speaks of "let[ting] the oppressed go free" (RSV). As we have seen above (chap. 6), this phrase deals with the revolution divinely programed for the Year of Jubilee.

Sight and Spiritual Vision. The third dimension of Jesus' praxis deals with his task to "proclaim . . . recovery of sight to the blind," who, as I have pointed out, represent all the sick. When John the Baptist was imprisoned, he sent messengers to Jesus to make sure that he was indeed the Messiah everyone was waiting for. Jesus answered:

> Go back and report to John what you have seen and heard: The blind receive sight, the lame walk, those who have leprosy are cured, the deaf hear, the dead are raised and the good news is preached to the poor. Blessed is the man who does not fall away on account of me [Luke 7:22-23].

That is, the mission of Jesus and his genuine followers always includes healing the sick, sometimes miraculously; happily, many churches are rediscovering this gift. We must not "spiritualize" our interpretation of Jesus' gospel to the point of eliminating or minimizing physical healing of diseases. But neither can we deny that the "sight" Jesus gives also sensitizes the human conscience. It provides a new spiritual discernment that sheds light on the human situation, especially on the sufferings of the poor.[9] This discernment can prod us not only into praying for the sick, but also into working, for example, for adequate health care for all citizens. As James says, "Faith without works is dead" (2:17).

"The Year of the Lord's Favor": Revolution. We can better understand the relationship between liberation and forgiveness by closely examining the final dimension in Jesus' message: "the year of the Lord's favor." Although this may not seem revolutionary at first glance, it is really the most revolutionary part of Jesus' message. It refers to the Year of Jubilee in Leviticus 25:8-55. According to this law, God had programed an out-and-out revolution into Israelite society every fifty years in order to avoid extremes of wealth and poverty among his people. Because this is a long and detailed piece of legislation, I shall not quote it in full; but it is important to grasp the three basic features of the Year of Jubilee. It provides for a repetition of the original exodus revolution every fifty years. The law's basic points are the following:

1) Liberty (manumission; Hebrew: *deror*) for all slaves and debtors: ". . . proclaim liberty throughout the land to all its inhabitants."[10] Obviously we have here a parallel to Israel's flight from Egypt recorded in Exodus.

2) The restitution of each clan's patrimony—a kind of agrarian reform accompanied by a redistribution of wealth: ". . . each one of you is to return to his family property and to his own clan."[11] This reminds us of the conquest of Canaan and equitable distribution of the land as described in Joshua.

3) Rest for the land, allowing it to lie fallow: ". . . do not sow, and do not reap what grows of itself."[12]

Clearly all the basic provisions of the law of Jubilee are related to freedom (of debtors, slaves, property, and even of the land). Thus Ezekiel simply referred to this time as "the year of freedom" (Ezek. 46:17). Isaiah, in the text

Jesus quoted, called it "the year of the Lord's favor" (Isa. 61:2). The Jubilee made Israel reexperience the events recorded in Exodus (freedom from slavery, departure from Egypt) and Joshua (the entrance into Canaan, an equitable distribution of land to each family). The Jubilee legislation was necessary because oppression of the poor was possible not only by foreign powers, but also by wealthy compatriots. The economic and social implications of the Year of Jubilee are revolutionary indeed. By faithfully following these laws, Israel would have avoided the extremes of wealth and poverty within its basically agricultural society.

We can rightly understand the Isaian text with which Jesus begins his ministry only by thinking of the Year of Jubilee. It is even possible that Jesus' ministry began in what would have been a Year of Jubilee according to the Jewish calendar.[13] In any case, the good news for the poor consists precisely in the arrival of the kingdom of God in Jesus' person, an event that puts into practice the provisions of the Year of Jubilee, or the year of the Lord's favor. We can see how throughout his ministry Jesus preached and taught his disciples how to practice the revolutionary provisions of Jubilee:

1) not by sowing, reaping, or harvesting, but by living by faith, always trusting that God will provide for one's needs: Luke 12:29–31; Matthew 6:25–26, 31–33.

2) by remitting all debts: Luke 6:33; 12:30–33; 16:1–15; Matthew 5:40–42; 6:12; 18:23–25.

3) by redistributing wealth: Luke 11:42; 12:30–33; Acts 2:44–45; 4:32–37.[14]

In this way Jesus continually stresses both the relationship between his ministry and the Year of Jubilee, and aspects of liberation that permeated his teaching and activities. For that reason Jesus combines in his own original way two Scripture texts (Isaiah 58:6 and 61:2) and so proclaims for all to hear that his mission starts the wheels of revolution rolling in the form of the Jubilee Year.[15]

MISSION AND PURPOSE OF THE CHRISTIAN

We have yet to answer the question: "What do true Christian commitment and praxis demand of someone today? I have seen what Jesus came to do, but what am I supposed to do?" Luke 4:18–19 suggests three steps in the Christian commitment. The first two prepare the way for the third, decisive step of genuine discipleship.

Self-Awareness

The first step is that I must become aware of my own situation in the light of God's attitude toward injustice.

Jesus spoke of the poor, the slaves, the sick, and the oppressed. I must recognize that this also faithfully describes my own personal condition. If that is not the case, Jesus has nothing to give me. As Jesus himself told the Pharisees (who considered themselves healthy and righteous):

It is not the healthy who need a doctor, but the sick. I have not come to call the righteous, but sinners [oppressors] to repentance [Luke 5:31-32].

All of us are simultaneously oppressed and oppressors (Acts 10:38; Rom. 3:23). Satanic oppression occurs not only on the level of economic class struggle, but in all areas of human life: in families, in schools, at the local fast-food restaurant—as also on the great landed estates and in the large multinational companies. The poor-oppressed workingman tyrannizes his wife and children more often than we might care to believe.

Thus the first step in genuine Christian discipleship is humbly to recognize my own situation: I am an oppressed oppressor. If I let pride and self-interest close my eyes to my own personal needs and faults, I will never be able to experience the liberation that Jesus offers. I can deceive neither God nor my friends—only myself: "If we claim to be without sin, we deceive ourselves and the truth is not in us" (1 John 1:8). Self-deception is the worst kind of blindness.

If I want to recognize my real situation, I must remember God's attitude to human injustice. Despite the fall, human beings are still made in the image of God. When I think about the injustice and oppression in the world, how do I feel? Angry?

If we feel that way, we can begin to imagine how God must feel. Paul says: "The wrath of God is being revealed from heaven against all the impiety and oppression of men" (Rom. 1:18). God's wrath is nothing like the capricious, irrational anger of the pagan deities. God's anger lashes out with moral indignation against selfishness, injustice, and oppression. Many Christians mistakenly conclude that because God is love, there is no such thing as divine anger. The Bible speaks otherwise. Precisely because God is love, he cannot remain indifferent to oppression of the poor (Exod. 22:21-24).

Jesus himself mirrored God's wrath against impiety and injustice when he cleansed the temple.[16] His anger also flashed against the Pharisees when they tried to oppose his liberating ministry.[17] That is just the way God is. The only book of the Bible that states "God is love" (1 John 4:8, 16) first states that "God is light" (holy, just, ready to strip off the subtle disguises of human egotism, 1 John 1:5). The same chapter in which we read "God so loved the world" finishes by declaring that "whoever rejects the Son will not see life, for God's wrath remains on him" (John 3:36; cf. v. 16). Liberation theologians have made an important contribution by articulating the conflictive nature of Christian love. As Giulio Girardi says in his work on Christian love and class conflict:

Of course the gospel commands us to love our enemies, but it does not tell us that we have no enemies or that we are not to struggle against them. . . . Christians must love everyone, but not in exactly the same way: they love the oppressed by defending them and liberating them; they love oppressors by laying charges against them and by struggling against them. Love demands that we struggle in order to free all who live in conditions of manifest sin. The liberation of the poor and of the rich occurs at exactly the same time. . . . In this way—paradoxically—class struggle does not contradict the universality of love; instead, that very struggle is one of love's demands.[18]

To put it another way, God loves us sinners but not our sins. However, in the face of all godlessness and human injustice God manifests his *anger*. As is evident from Exodus, God's struggle on behalf of the oppressed requires political involvement, but does not require violent means.[19] Here we encounter the Bible's most profound analysis of the human situation: What does the liberation that Jesus proclaims have to do with God's anger?

Once again we find an answer in the references that Jesus made to the Year of Jubilee. This in turn will lead us to the second step in the process of becoming Jesus' true disciple.

Awareness of Jesus

I must recognize who Jesus is and what he did to liberate me. The good news that Jesus came to proclaim to the poor finds its focus in Jesus' own person and in what he came to do.

In the history of human thought we may discover many liberating truths in the works of such thinkers as Plato, Aristotle, Buddha, Thomas Aquinas, Luther, Darwin, Freud, Marx, Engels, and many others. But only Jesus could affirm, "I am the truth" (John 14:6). He insisted, "If the Son sets you free, you will be free indeed" (John 8:36).

Jesus could say that about himself only because he is God the Son, our creator (John 1:1, 2). He was born a human being into an oppressive situation; he fully identified with the poor, and hence laid the foundation for total human liberation—starting with the poor. He withstood every one of the devil's temptations by living without selfish interests. He fought against alienation in his society—its racism, nationalism, and chauvinism; he advanced woman's liberation (John 4). Though he was not a politician, he made the religious leaders, the local political oligarchy of his day, shake in their sandals! They finally managed to crucify him without realizing that God had planned to use the crucifixion as the foundation for total human liberation (Acts 2:23). In the face of the oligarchy's unjust violence, God unleashed an all-powerful counterforce: the resurrection of the Son (Col. 2:5).

Why did Jesus have to die? To appreciate this most profound dimension of the liberation that Jesus provides, we turn once more to the Year of Jubilee in Leviticus 25.

We must recall *when* the Jubilee occurred in Israel's calendar. As we read in Leviticus, "On the Day of Atonement *(kopher)* sound the trumpet throughout the land" (25:9). Jubilee is built on the Day of Atonement, which God used to foreshadow the ultimate sacrifice, that of his own Son.

That is how Paul would have us understand Jesus' death. We find the root of the human problem set forth in Romans 1:18 where God's wrath strikes out against all godlessness and human injustice. Paul explains the meaning of the death of Jesus:

> [whom] God presented . . . as a propitiation through faith in his blood. He did this to demonstrate justice, because in his forbearance he had left the sins committed beforehand unpunished—he did it to demonstrate his justice at the present time after the cross, so as to be just and the one who justifies the man who has faith in Jesus [3:25–26].[20]

When we compare the Bible passages we see a clearly drawn parallel:

(a) In Leviticus the Jubilee is built on the Day of Atonement.
(b) In Luke 4:18–19 liberation is connected with forgiveness.
(c) In Romans liberation is established through propitiation in which Jesus' blood wards off God's anger.

That is, the cross of Jesus stands as a cosmic lightning rod: on the cross God's son suffered hell and all other consequences of God's anger over human injustice. In the following chapters of Romans, Paul shows us how all the dimensions of our liberation flow from the cross of Christ:

(a) We are justified—freed from the *guilt of sin* (3–4);
(b) freed from *God's wrath* (5:9; cf., 1 Thess. 5:9);
(c) freed from the power of *sin* (6:18);
(d) freed from the *law* (7:6);
(e) freed from *death* (8:2).

Full Christian freedom is built on Jesus' propitiatory death. As a crowning touch, Christ will free the entire creation from corruption and death (Rom. 8:21).

In this way we can better appreciate the context of Jesus' statement in Luke 4:18–19. Already at his baptism Jesus committed himself to follow the way of the cross. When he was tempted, he firmly withstood all the satanic stratagems that would have lured him from that path.[21] For that reason, having once chosen the way of the cross and anticipating that he would perform the only sacrifice that could turn away God's wrath, he could begin his ministry by proclaiming (as the trumpet that launched the Year of Jubilee) "good news for the poor" and "freedom for the prisoners."

We now have examined what Jesus did to make our full liberation possible. But what do I have to do in order to benefit from this liberation? One more step remains.

Commitment

I must commit myself personally to Jesus. Do I recognize Jesus as the only true liberator? I must personally trust in him as my liberator and firmly step into the ranks of his followers.

Do I recognize that I am bound by selfishness, by vices; alienated from God? Do I admit that, of myself, I am incapable of promoting justice and authentic human liberation? It is not enough that those who are slaves to such forces struggle against their bonds: God's Son must set us free! All kinds of human philosophies and religions *talk about* liberation, but only Jesus offers himself as the liberator who is fully able to free us.

I must not put my trust in other "liberations" and "liberators," be they education, humanistic sciences, non-Christian religious superstitions (spiritism, witchcraft, astrology, political ideologies, etc.). I must trust only and completely in Jesus as my liberator; he is the one who frees me from the control of selfishness, from God's wrath now and in the future.

Jesus can liberate us from anything because he is "Lord of all" (Acts 10:36). That Jesus is Lord is an intrinsic element of the good news. As he himself announced after having conquered death: "All authority has been given me in heaven and on earth" (Matt. 28:18).

Therefore no other power can threaten us, bind us, or make us afraid. As Paul exults:

> No, in all these things we are more than conquerors through him who loved us. For I am convinced that neither death nor life, neither angels nor demons, neither the present nor the future, nor any powers, neither height nor depth, nor anything else in all creation, will be able to separate us from the love of God that is in Christ Jesus our Lord [Rom. 8:37-39].

In order to enjoy this complete freedom from alienating powers, I must personally and consciously turn myself over to Jesus by recognizing him as the Lord of my life. I must say:

> Make me a captive, Lord, and then I shall be free;
> Force me to render up my sword, and I shall conqueror be.[22]

I am by nature an individualistic rebel. Something in me makes me not want to recognize Jesus' authority over my life. This is the heart of the human problem, according to the Scriptures:

We all, like sheep, have gone astray, each of us has turned to his own way; and the Lord has laid on him the iniquity of us all [Isa. 53:6].

But the liberation that Christ offers is not license. In order to experience genuine freedom and in order to be an instrument of freedom, I must turn my back on selfishness and individualism and place my life in the hands of my Creator. Only my Creator can free me from every vice. Only my Creator can cleanse, fill, and guide my life in such a way that it becomes an abundant life used to free others.

Appendix

Open Letter to North American Christians

September 11, 1977

Dear Brothers and Sisters in Christ:

As Latin American Christians we are shocked at the opposition of so many United States citizens to the new Panama Canal treaty. Your press provides ample coverage of the historical and diplomatic factors that have prompted your government to negotiate a new treaty, so we do not propose to rehash the arguments.

However, inasmuch as you have sent thousands of missionaries to Latin America, telling us to study and obey the Bible as God's word, we should like to point out three passages of Scripture that we see as particularly relevant to the new treaty.

1) *The story of Naboth's vineyard (1 Kings 21)*. Ahab, a wealthy king, was not content with his riches, but coveted the vineyard of poor Naboth, that it might serve as the royal vegetable garden. Naboth protested, "The Lord forbid that I should give you the inheritance of my fathers" (v. 3). When Naboth refused to sell his vineyard, Queen Jezebel devised a wicked scheme to secure the vineyard for her husband.

The United States wanted a canal in Panama for the benefit of its growing industries. To secure its ends, it fomented a rebellion, established a puppet government, and imposed an unjust treaty on the newly created nation—a treaty never signed by a Panamanian and never approved of by the Panamanian people, who for seventy years have protested, "The Lord forbid that I should sell you the inheritance of my father." The new treaty, correcting some of the grosser injustices in the original, is long overdue and deserves the support of the Christian public.

2) *Nathan's parable (2 Samuel 12)*. King David had many wives, but in a moment of weakness committed adultery with Bathsheba, the wife of Uriah, and then had Uriah killed to cover up his crime. God sent Nathan the prophet

with a parable about a rich man, with many flocks and herds, who stole the one little ewe lamb of a poor man. David angrily declared that the man who did such a thing deserved to die. Nathan said, "You are the man."

Panama is a poor nation: its only natural resource of any great value is the narrow stretch of land that the United States took over for the canal. You did not "buy it"—you stole it. And although you proclaim the virtues of free enterprise, you have imposed extremely low rates on canal traffic throughout this century, saving billions in shipping costs for U.S.A. businesses (and those of other nations)—all at the expense of Panama. It is time to begin to correct this injustice and let Panama share in some of the benefits of the free enterprise you preach. How would you feel if the French had managed to get control of the Mississippi River and the states bordering it, in exchange for their support of your revolution?

3) *The Year of Jubilee (Leviticus 25)*. Jesus made this the basis of his own proclamation of the "good news to the poor" (Luke 4:18–19). It stipulates that at the end of fifty years all properties of the poor that have fallen under the control of the rich are to be restored to their original owners. By this provision God legislated against the development of extreme wealth and poverty in Israel.

The year 1964 marked the Jubilee year from the inauguration of the canal in 1914. The United States refused to rectify its dishonest and unjust treatment of Panama. Violence broke out, leaving twenty Panamanian students and four of your marines dead. Had you followed the Jubilee teaching of Moses, the prophets, and Jesus, this violence would have been averted. As one of your biblical scholars concludes: "Applied to nations, the principles underlying the Jubilee condemn permanent colonialism and unbridled exploitation of the soil to the detriment of its inhabitants" (*Interpreter's Dictionary of the Bible: Supplementary Volume* [Abingdon Press, 1976], p. 498).

Inscribed on your Liberty Bell are words from the biblical Jubilee laws. Recently you celebrated the 200th anniversary of your own liberation from British colonialism. Panama has waited patiently while you procrastinated in the renegotiation of the treaty through the years of Vietnam, Watergate, and the recent elections. You condemn the vestiges of colonialism in white racist rule in Rhodesia and South Africa. Why are you so slow to see the "beam in your own eye"?

During the construction of the canal, more than twenty-five thousand poor laborers from the Third World laid down their lives on the altar of First World economic development—yet your politicians have the gall to boast "*we* built it"! Your founding fathers never intended the greatness of the United States to be as a colonial power, but as an example to the world of a nation that seeks to "do justice, to love mercy, and to walk humbly with your God" (Micah 6:8). Your senators have been swamped with letters from citizens blinded by ignorance, greed, and ethnocentrism. We exhort you as brothers and sisters in Christ to write your senators today, indicating your support for the new treaty as a step toward justice for Panama and better relations with all Latin America.

Sincerely in our Lord,

Members, Professional Group,
Agrupación Universitaria Cristiana
(I.F.E.S./Inter-Varsity)
San José, Costa Rica

Notes

CHAPTER 1

1. *Theology for a Nomad Church* (Maryknoll, N.Y.: Orbis, 1976), pp. 37–38, 49, 52–54. Idem, *Pueblo oprimido, Señor de la historia* (Montevideo: Tierra Nueva, 1972).

2. *'Ashaq*: Ludwig Koehler and Walter Baumgartner, *Lexicon in Veteris Testamenti Libros* (Leiden: Brill, 2nd ed., 1958), p. 744; hereafter, KB². Francis Brown, S. R. Driver, and Charles A. Briggs, *A Hebrew and English Lexicon of the Old Testament* (Oxford: Clarendon, 1907), pp. 798 ff.; hereafter, BDB. William L. Holladay, ed., *A Concise Hebrew and Aramaic Lexicon of the Old Testament* (Grand Rapids: Eerdmans, 1971, p. 286; hereafter, Hol. In the italicized texts following, poverty occurs in the context with oppression as its evident cause.

'Ashaq (verb): Lev. 5:21, 23 [6:2, 4]; 19:13; *Deut. 24:14; 28:29, 33;* 1 Sam. 12:3, 4; 1 Chron. 16:21; Job 10:3; [35:9 cj]; 40:23; *Ps. 72:4; 103:6;* 105:14 (// 1 Chron. 16:21); *119:121, 122; 146:7; Prov. 14:31; 22:16; 28:3,* 17; Ecclus. 4:1 (twice); *Isa.* 23:12; *52:4; Jer. 7:6; 21:12; 50:33; Ezek. 18:18; 22:29* (twice); *Hos.* 5:11; *12:8[7]; Amos 4:1; Mic. 2:2; Zech. 7:10; Mal. 3:5.* Total, 37 times.

'Osheq (noun): Lev. 5:23 [6:4]; Isa. 30:12; 54:14; 59:13; *Jer. 6:6; 22:17; Ezek. 18:18; 22:7, 12,29;* Ps. 62:11[10]; 73:8; *119:134; Ecclus. 5:7;* 7:7. Total, 15 times.

'Oshqah: Isa. 38:14; *'ashoq: Jer. 22:3; 'ashuqim:* Job 35:9; Ecclus. 4:1; Amos 3:9; *ma'ashaqoth: Isa.33:15; Prov. 28:16.* Total, 7 times.

Total, 59 times (31 with poverty; italicized references).

In her study of the mechanisms of oppression, Elsa Tamez stresses the common link between *'ashaq* and *gazel* ("rob"): *Bible of the Oppressed* (Maryknoll, N.Y.: Orbis, 1982), p. 23.

3. Expressions such as these make it difficult to believe that Solomon could be the author of the book, because the main responsibility of the king in Israel was to defend the rights of the oppressed (see, e.g., Ps. 72). See also Edward J. Young, *An Introduction to the Old Testament* (Grand Rapids: Eerdmans, 1949), pp. 339–44.

4. "El pueblo de Dios y la liberación del hombre," *Fichas de ISAL*, 3 (1970): 9 f. See also Ambrosias F. Lenssen, *La salida de Egipto en la Biblia* (Estella: Ed. Verbo Divino, 1971).

5. *Yanah*: KB², p. 385; BDB, p. 413; Hol., p. 136. *Exod. 22:20; Lev. 19:33; 25:14, 17; Deut. 23:17[16]; Isa. 49:26; Jer. 22:3;* 25:38; 46:16; 50:16; *Ezek. 18: 7, 12, 16; 22:7, 29; 45:8; 46:18;* Zeph. 3:1; *Ps. 74:8;* [123:4 cj].

Total, 20 times (15 with poverty). Tamez stresses violence and robbery as mechanisms of oppression commonly associated with this root: *Bible of the Oppressed*, pp. 27–28.

6. Gerhard von Rad, *Deuteronomy: A Commentary* (Philadelphia: Westminster, 1966), p. 147.

7. *Nagas:* KB², p. 594; BDB, p. 620; Hol., p. 227. *Exod. 3:7; 5:6, 10, 13, 14* [all J source]; *Deut. 15:2, 3; 1 Sam. 13:6; 14:24; 2 Kings 23:35; Isa. 3:5,12; 9:3[4];* 14:2, 4; *53:7; 58:3; 60:17; Zech. 9:8; 10:4; Dan. 11:20; Job 3:18;* 39:7.

Total, 23 times (20 with poverty). See Tamez, *Bible of the Oppressed*, pp. 9–11.

8. *Lahats* (verb): KB², pp. 479 f.; BDB, p. 537 f.; Hol., p. 176. *Exod. 3:9; 22:20[21]; 23:9;* Num. 22:25 (twice) [24:8 cj.]; *Judg.* 1:34; *2:18;* 4:3; *6:9;* 10:12; *1 Sam. 10:18;* 2 Kings 6:32; *13:4,* 22; Isa. 19:20; Jer. 30:20; *Amos 6:14;* Ps. 56:2[1]; 106:42.

Lahats (noun): *Exod. 3:9; Deut. 26:7; 1 Kings 22:27* (twice); *2 Kings 13:4; 2 Chron. 18:26* (twice); *Isa. 30:20;* Ps. 42:10[9]; 43:2; *44:25[24]; Job 36:15.*

Total, 31 times (17 with poverty). Tamez elaborates well the relationship of *lahats* to the cries for liberation: *Bible of the Oppressed*, pp. 15–17.

9. On the close relation between compassion and justice in biblical theology, see J. Verkuyl, "The Calling of North Atlantic Churches and Christians in Relation to the Issues of Domination and Dependence" in *To Break the Chains of Oppression*, Julio de Santa Ana, ed. (Geneva: World Council of Churches, 1975), p. 93.

10. *Ratsats:* KB², p. 908; BDB, p. 954; Hol., p. 346. Gen. 25:22; *Deut. 28:33; Judg.* 9:53; *10:8;* 1 Sam. 12:3, 4; 2 Kings 18:21; 23:12; *2 Chron. 16:10; Isa.* 36:6; *42:3, 4; 58:6;* Ezek. 29:7; *Hos. 5:11; Amos 4:1; Job 20:19;* Ps. 74:14; Eccl. 12:6 (twice).

Total, 20 times (9 with poverty). See Tamez, *Bible of the Oppressed*, pp. 28–29.

11. Edward J. Young, *The Book of Isaiah* (Grand Rapids: Eerdmans, 1971), vol. 3, pp. 113–14; Claus Westermann, *Isaiah 40–66: A Commentary* (Philadelphia: Westminster, 1969), pp. 92–97.

12. Young, *Isaiah,* p. 114.

13. For more details on Isa. 58, see chap. 5, 6, and 7, below; also John Howard Yoder, *The Politics of Jesus* (Grand Rapids: Eerdmans, 1972), pp. 64–77.

14. Ronald J. Sider, *Rich Christians in an Age of Hunger* (Downers Grove, Ill.: InterVarsity, 1977), p. 137. It is this insensitive *isolation* of the rich from the reality of the life of the poor that James (1:27) seeks to combat with his insistence on a praxis involving regularly visiting oppressed classes. Only thus, he concludes, will our "religion" be authentic (not an opiate). On James 1:27 see below, chap. 3.

15. Ibid., p. 137.

16. *Daka':* KB², p. 209; BDB, pp. 193 f.; Hol., p. 70. Job 4:19; 5:4; 6:9; 19:2; 22:9; 34:25; *Ps.72:4; 89:11[10]; 94:5;* 143:3; *Prov. 22:22;* Lam. 3:34; *Isa. 3:15;* 19:10; *53:5,10;* 57:15; Jer. 44:10. Total, 18 times.

Dakā': Ps. 34:19[18]; 90:3; Isa. 57:15. Total, 3 times.

Dakah: Ps.10:10; 38:9[8]; 44:20[19]; 51:10, 19[8, 17]. Total, 5 times.

Dakāh: Deut. 23:2. Once.

Daki: Ps. 93:3. Once.

Dak: Ps. 9:10[9]; 10:18; 74:21; [Ps. 10:12 cj; Prov. 26:28 cj]. Total, 3 times.

Total, 31 times (10 with poverty). See Tamez, *Bible of the Oppressed*, pp. 26–27.

17. Hans-Joachim Kraus, *Psalmen BKAT,* vol. 1 (Neukirchen-Vluyn: Neukirchener Verlag, 5th ed., 1978), p. 232. See also his excursus on the poor, pp.108–11.

18. *'anah:* KB², p. 719; BDB, p. 776; Hol., pp. 277 f.

Qal: Isa. 31:4; Zech. 10:2; Ps. 116:10; 119:67; Eccl. 1:13; 3:10; Lam. 4:3.

Nifil: *Isa. 53:7;* Job 22:23; Exod. 10:3; *Isa. 58:10;* Ps. 119:107; [Judg. 16:19 cj.].

Piel: *Gen. 15:3;* 16:6; 31:50; 34:2; *Exod. 1:11, 12; 22:21, 22[22, 23];* Lev. 16:29, 31; 23:27, 32; Num. 24:24; 29:7; 30:14; Deut. 8:2, 3, 16; 21:14; 22:24, 29; *26:6;* Judg. 16:5, 6, 19; 19:24; 20:5; [1 Sam. 12:8 cj]; 2 Sam. 7:10; 13:12, 14, 22, 32; 1 Kings 11:39; 2 Kings 17:20; *Isa. 58:3, 5;* 60:14; 64:11; Ezek. 22:10,11; *Nah. 1:12* (twice); *Zeph. 3:19;*

Ps. 35:13; 88:8[7]; 89:23[22]; 90:15; *94:5;* 102:24Q[23]; 105:18Q; 119:75; Job 30:11Q; 37:23; Lam. 3:33; 5:11.

Pual: *Isa. 53:4;* Ps. 119:71; 132:1; Lev. 23:29.

Hifil: 1 Kings 8:35; Isa. 25:5; Ps. 55:20; 2 Chron. 6:26.

Hithpael: Gen. 16:9; 1 Kings 2:26 (twice); Dan. 10:12; Ezra 8:21; Ps. 107:17.

Total, 82 times (14 with poverty). See Tamez, *Bible of the Oppressed*, pp. 11-15.

19. H.C. Leupold observes: "To make the whole sojourn one continuous oppression is completely at variance with the facts" (*Exposition of Genesis* [Columbus, Ohio: Wartburg, 1942], p. 484). Most commentaries do not mention the problem, much less resolve it. However, the Hebrew phrase "400 years" is separated from the previous words by the accent that usually indicates the major division of the verse. Therefore, the words "400 years" could be a later chronological note meant to describe the entire time in Egypt—not just the years of oppression.

20. On the extensive Old Testament vocabulary for divine anger (some 45 words), in addition to the standard theological dictionaries—all very incomplete—see my thesis: "The Theology of Divine Anger in the Psalms of Lament" (St. Louis: Concordia Seminary, 1972).

21. KB², p. 720; Hol., p. 278.

22. BDB, pp. 864 f.; KB², pp. 815, 818; Hol., pp. 310 f.

ᵘ*Tsar:* Gen. 14:20; Num. 10:9; 24:8; Deut. 32:27, 41, 43; 33:7; Josh. 5:13; 2 Sam. 24:13; Isa. 1:24; 9:10; 26:11; 59:18; 63:18; 64:1; Jer. 30:16; 46:10; 48:5; 50:7; Ezek. 30:16; 39:23; Amos 3:11; Mic. 5:8; Nah. 1:2; *Zech. 8:10;* Ps. 3:2; 13:35; 27:2, 12; 44:6, 8, 11; 60:13, 14; 74:10; 78:42, 61, 66; 81:15; 89:24, 43; 97:3; 105:24; 106:11; 107:2; 108:13, 14; 112:8; *119:139, 157; 136:24;* Job 6:23; 16:9; 19:11; *Lam. 1:*5 (twice), 7 (twice), *10,*17; 2:4, 17; 4:12; Esther 7:6; Ezra. 4:1; Neh. 4:5; 9:27 (twice); 1 Chron. 12:18; 21:12. Total, 70 times (6 with poverty).

ᵘ*Tsarar:* Exod. 23:22; Lev. 18:18; Num. 10:9; 25:17, 18; 33:55; Isa. 11:13; *Amos 5:12;* Ps. 6:8; 7:5, 7; 8:3; 10:5; 23:5; 31:12; 42:11; *69:20[19];* 74:4, *23;* 129:1, 2; 143:12; Esther 3:10; 8:1; 9:10, 24. Total, 26 times (3 with poverty).

Total, 96 times (9 with poverty).

23. BDB, pp. 864 f.; KB², pp. 815, 818; Hol., pp. 310 f.

ᴵ*Tsarar:* Gen. 32:8; Deut. 4:30; 28:52 (twice); Josh. 9:4; *Judg. 2:15;* 10:9; 11:7; 1 Sam. 13:16; 28:15; 30:6; 2 Sam. 1:26; 13:2; 22:7; 24:14; 1 Kings 8:37; *Isa. 25:4;* 28:20; 49:19; Jer. 10:18; 48:41; 49:22; Hos. 5:15; Zeph. 1:17; *Ps.* 18:7; *31:10;* 59:17; 66:14; 69:18; 102:3; 106:44; *107:6, 13,* 19, 28; Job 18:7; 20:22; Prov. 4:12; Lam. 1:20; Neh. 9:27; 1 Chron. 21:13; 2 Chron. 6:28; 15:4; 28:20, 22; 33:12. Total, 46 times (5 with poverty).

ᴵ*Tsar:* Num. 22:26; 2 Kings 6:1; Isa. 5:30; 26:16; 30:20; 49:20; 63:9; Ps. 4:2; 32:7; 119:143; Job 7:11; 15:24; 36:16, 19; 38:23; Prov. 23:27; 24:10; [cj: 1 Sam. 2:32; Isa. 59:19; Job 41:7; Esther 7:6]. Total 17 times (plus 4 cj).

ᴵ*Tsarah:* Gen. 35:3; 42:21 (twice); Deut. 31:17, 21; Judg. 10:14; 1 Sam. 10:19; 26:24; 2 Sam. 4:9; 1 Kings 1:29; 2 Kings 19:3; *Isa. 8:22;* 30:6; 33:2; 37:3; 46:7; 63:9(Q); 65:16; Jer. 4:31; 6:24; 14:8; 15:11; 16:19; 30:7; 49:24; 50:43; Obad. 12, 14; Jon. 2:3; Nah. 1:7, 9; Hab. 3:16; Zeph. 1:15; Zech. 10:11; *Ps.* 20:2; 22:12; *25:17; 31:8; 34:7[6],* 18[17]; 37:39; 46:2; 50:15; 54:9; 71:20; 77:3; 78:49; 81:8; *86:7;* 91:15; 116:3; 120:1; 138:7; 142:3; 143:11; Job 5:19; 27:9; Prov. 1:27; 11:8; 12:13; 17:17; 21:23; 24:10; 25:19; Dan. 12:1; Neh. 9:27, 37; 2 Chron. 15:6; 20:9. Total, 69 times (5 with poverty).

Total, 132 times (10 with poverty). I recognize that in examining the uses of these words we should not let the "meaning" of each word grow like a snowball, accumulating new senses with each use. This would confuse the meaning with the things to which it refers. James Barr gives the example of the Hebrew *maqom* ("place"), which at times refers to a tomb. He says that we ought not conclude from this fact that the word *means* tomb (*Comparative Philology and the Text of the Old Testament* [Oxford: Clarendon, 1968], p. 292). On the other hand, the distinction is not always simple to maintain. Continual reference may affect meaning. In Nicaragua, before the revolution, *El hombre* ("The man") referred to Somoza (unnameable terror!). At what point does a common referent become part of the acceptable meaning? In addition to "linguistic oppression" (see *"Thlĩpsis*: The Lexicons and the Translations," chap. 3, below), we also have linguistic "revolutions," where a common referent "takes over" a word and traditional meanings fall into disuse.

24. *Tsuq, tsoq, tsuqah, mutsaq, motsoq,* "*metsuqah:* KB², pp. 798 f., 556, 505; Hol. 304, 210 f., 187.

Tsuq: Deut. 28:53, 55, 57; Judg. 14:17; 16:16; Job 32:18; Isa. 29:2, 7; 51:13 (twice); Jer. 19:9. Total, 11 times (3 with poverty).

Tsoq: Dan. 9:25 (once).

Tsuqah: Isa. 8:22; 30:6; Prov. 1:27. Total, 3 times (1 with poverty).

Mutsaq: Isa. 8:23; Job 36:16; 37:10. Total, 3 times (2 with poverty).

Motsoq: Deut. 28:53, 55, 57; 1 Sam. 22:2; Jer. 19:9; Ps. 119:143. Total, 6 times (3 with poverty).

Metsuqah: Zeph. 1:15; Job 15:24; *Ps. 25:17; 107:6, 13, 19, 28.* Total, 5 times (4 with poverty).

Total, 31 times (14 with poverty).

25. Young, *Isaiah,* vol. 1, p. 327.

26. Ibid., p. 325.

27. Ibid., p. 344.

28. Joyce G. Baldwin, *Daniel* (Downers Grove, Ill.: InterVarsity, 1978), pp. 168–78.

29. Scholars concerned with the biblical bases for Latin American liberation theologies are well advised to read the published version of a doctoral dissertation submitted to the Faculté Libre de Théologie Protestante de Paris (1975): Jacques Pons, *L'oppression dans l'Ancien Testament* (Paris: Letouzey et Ané, 1981). The major overlap with my own investigation occurs in the study of basic Hebrew roots for "oppression." Working with the rigorous technical linguistic and critical methodology expected in a European doctoral dissertation, Pons ably sharpens our understanding of the distinctive connotations of the terms *'sq ('ashaq), ynh (yanah), rṣṣ (ratsats), lḥṣ (lahats), 'nh ('anah), ngś (nagas)* (pp. 67–109). Whereas I count 10 basic Hebrew roots, Pons counts only these 6, plus *hamas* and *šdd* (pp. 53–66), which I do not consider basic. His study does include brief references to the 4 other roots I consider basic: *daka'* (pp. 102, 155–56), '*tsarar,* "*tsarar* (148, 155, 164–65), and *tsuq* (pp. 24, 162, 167, 197). He also makes passing references to 4 of what I consider the 10 less frequent roots: *dhq, hamots, 'oster,* and *'etser.* In the second part of his work, Pons studies the Greek translations (esp. the LXX) of the Hebrew vocabulary for "oppression," which goes beyond the scope of my investigation and fills an obvious gap. This section could prove the most important for future studies because it lays the foundation for an entirely new interpretation of the New Testament teaching on oppression and liberation. In his third section Pons gives a helpful survey of oppression in the ancient Near East. This should prove a fruitful starting point for more rigorous studies by linguistic experts in several fields, especially in conjunction with more recent discoveries such as the Ebla texts just now becoming available. The Pons work is very important for correcting ideological biases in our existing lexicons, translations, commentaries, and theologies.

CHAPTER 2

1. Perhaps the most popular book on fasting in pentecostal and charismatic circles is that of Arthur Wallis, *God's Chosen Fast* (Fort Washington, Pa.: Christian Literature Crusade, 1968). Wallis even takes his title from Isa. 58:6 and devotes a key chapter (pp. 48–52) to expounding Isa. 58. But, alas, instead of faithful exegesis we are treated at this point to flights of Platonic spiritualizing (p. 48) in terms of exorcism! The literal sense is recognized and affirmed: "The primary reference is of course to literal slavery" (p. 51). However, "if this word does not have a literal explication for us who live in lands where there is little to be seen of the grosser forms of social injustice [1968!], it surely has an application in the spiritual realm" (p. 48). Latin American theologians would suggest that the "exorcism" most needed is that of First World exegetes and Bible expositors! The frenetic flight from the literal sense of biblical texts on oppression and poverty often appears to take us back to medievial allegorizing. For all that, Wallis's book, aside from the small defect of having missed completely the basic biblical meaning and significance of fasting, may be the best popular study available on a most unpopular subject. For a perceptive treatment on spiritualizing in the history of biblical interpretation, see Pablo Leggett, *¿Platon o Jesucristo?* (San José: Seminario Bíblico Latinoamericano). For starters in English, see Ranald Macauley and Jerram Barrs, *Being Human* (Downers Grove, Ill.: InterVarsity, 1978), pp. 29–59.

2. Derek Kidner, *The Proverbs* (London: Tyndale, 1964), p. 175. See William McKane, *Proverbs* (Philadelphia: Westminster, 1970), p. 257, for details on our translation of the text.

3. Kraus, *Psalmen*, vol. 2, p. 1082.

4. *Psalms 73–105* (London: Inter-Varsity, 1975), p. 459.

5. *Isaiah*, vol. 1, p. 72.

6. Ibid., p. 73.

7. Ibid., p. 74.

8. José P. Miranda, *Marx and the Bible: A Critique of the Philosophy of Oppression* (Maryknoll, N.Y.: Orbis, 1974), p. 100. This important study—really of the biblical theology of justice—is also a goldmine for exegetical and theological perspectives on oppression. The catchy title, which undoubtedly helped make it quite popular in Latin America, may have scared off most First World biblical scholars. Although sometimes extreme in its conclusions, it is carefully researched, perceptive, and highly creative. Regarding the "wicked" in the psalms, Miranda's conclusion receives additional support from A. A. Anderson, who comments on Ps. 59: "It is very likely that the four different terms for evil-doers in verses 1–2 are synonymous, and refer to the oppressors in general" (*Psalms* [New Century Bible, London: Oliphants, 1972], vol. 1, p. 435). The Hebrew words are *'oyeb* ("enemies"); *qwm* ("those who *rise up* against me"); *po'ale 'awen* ("doers of iniquity"); *'anashey damim* ("men of blood"). See also Anderson's comment on *dll*, "bring low, oppress" (Ps. 116:6; Judg. 6:6): *Psalms*, vol. 2, p. 792 (Hol., p. 71).

9. Miranda, *Marx*, pp. 88–89. He also says (p. 83): "As Hertzberg, Zimmerli, and Westermann observe, the entire message of Deutero-Isaiah (40–55) is a response on the part of Yahweh to the cry of an oppressed people."

10. Norman K. Gottwald, *The Tribes of Yahweh: A Sociology of the Religion of Liberated Israel, 1250–1050 B.C.E.* (Maryknoll, N.Y.: Orbis, 1979), p. 531. Gottwald, following G. E. Mendenhall, argues that the exodus group from Egypt served as a

catalyst to *'apiru* and other oppressed-poor slave and peasant types already in Canaan, sparking a kind of peasant revolution against the oppressive oligarchy (see especially Shechem, Josh. 24, not conquered or destroyed by Joshua). Few have the technical training in both Old Testament and sociology to properly evaluate the kind of methodology and evidence Gottwald presents.

11. John W. Wenham, *The Goodness of God* (Downers Grove: InterVarsity, 1974), pp. 119-47.

12. Pablo Richard, "Nuestra lucha es contra los ídolos," in *La lucha de los dioses* (San José: DEI, 1980), p. 10; cf. p.18 (English translation, *The Idols of Death and the God of Life* [Maryknoll, N.Y.: Orbis, 1983]). Of course, inasmuch as about 90 percent of biblical history is written from the perspective of a poor- oppressed nation, the majority of biblical texts on almost any theme occur in a context of struggle against oppression! Still Richard's discussion of texts pointing to the link between idolatry and oppression is revealing: Exod. 32; 1 Kings 12:26-33; 21; 2 Kings 21; Jer. 10; Isa. 44:9-20; 46:1-7. Richard stresses certain prophetic texts that liberal higher critics have tended to neglect theologically because they are commonly viewed as "inauthentic" later additions to the prophetic books. Taken as inspired *relecturas*, they recapture their canonical authority!

13. Leon Morris, *The Cross in the New Testament* (Grand Rapids: Eerdmans, 1965). Wolfhart Pannenberg, *Jesus—God and Man* (London: SCM Press, 1968), pp. 278-80.

14. Jürgen Moltmann, *El Dios Crucificado* (Salamanca: Sígueme, 1975), pp. 333 ff.; in English, *The Crucified God* (New York: Harper & Row, 1974).

15. See also the full identification by faith of the justified with his substitute in Galatians: "I have been crucified with Christ and I no longer live, but Christ lives in me. . . ." That is, the substitution has a double context of identification: Christ identifies with oppressed humanity through his incarnation, and they by faith with him. Because of the unique, complex nature of the reality described (identification-substitution-identification), whatever human analogy—such as a judge who takes the punishment of his condemned—can be only partial and limited. Therefore, the moral arguments against penal substitution only demonstrate the inadequacy of the human analogies: their force utterly disappears when the total complex reality of Christ's work is taken into account.

16. 1 Cor. 1:17-18, 12; 2:2, etc.

17. See Gerhard von Rad, *Old Testament Theology* (Edinburgh: Oliver and Boyd, 1965), vol. 2, p. 376. C. F. D. Moule asks why there are not even more references in the New Testament to Isa. 53 (there are seven direct citations). However, he does not take into account sufficiently the allusions and heavy use of the concepts (*The Birth of the New Testament* [New York: Harper & Row, 1962], pp. 81-83). See R. T. France, *Jesus and the Old Testament* (London: Tyndale, 1971), pp. 110-32, for more detailed treatment.

18. Karl Barth, for instance, mentions in passing "secret or blatant oppression and exploitation of one's fellow"—in the course of an 80-page treatment of "The Sloth of Man"! Perhaps, like Billy Graham, he read Proverbs too much. The proportion might well have been reversed (*Church Dogmatics*, IV:2 [Edinburgh: Clark, 1958], p. 436; cf. pp. 403-83).

19. Revolution in the military sense (which is really the height of conformity) should not of course be romanticized, as Jacques Ellul makes devastatingly clear (*Autopsy of Revolution* [New York: Knopf, 1971]; *The Betrayal of the West* [New York: Seabury, 1978]). However, the peculiar U.S. penchant for deliriously celebrating each year our own revolution—while condemning as diabolical communist plots all similar efforts in

Latin America to break the yoke of colonialism and feudalism—can hardly be viewed as Christian or biblical. For another perspective, see Jon Sobrino, "Dios y los procesos revolucionarios" in *Apuntes para una teología nicaragüence* (San José: DEI, 1981), pp. 105-29; also Vernon C. Grounds, *Revolution and the Christian Faith* (Philadelphia: Lippincott, 1971); Francis A. Schaeffer, *A Christian Manifesto* (Westchester, Ill.: Crossway Books, 1981), pp. 94-130.

CHAPTER 3

1. *The Liberation of Theology* (Maryknoll, N.Y.: Orbis, 1976), p. 7.

2. *Biblia y Liberación* (Bogotá: Ed. Paulinas, 1976), p. 11.

3. We may compare the first of two preconditions that Segundo considers necessary for a hermeneutic circle: "that the questions rising out of the present be rich enough, general enough, and basic enough to force us to change our customary conceptions of life, death, knowledge, society, politics, and the world in general" (*Liberation*, p. 8).

4. See David H. Kelsey, *The Uses of Scripture in Recent Theology* (Philadelphia: Fortress, 1975), p. 23. I do not believe James Barr is fair to Warfield when he treats him as a kind of scapegoat for all that has gone bad in conservative theology. Although Charles Hodge continued to represent the kind of dogmatic theology typical of the seventeenth-century (F. Turretin; proof texting), in Warfield we begin to breathe the fresh air of biblical theology. This is true even in the case of Warfield's famous writings about inspiration, and even more so in his other works, which Barr does not take into account (*Fundamentalism* [London: SCM Press, 1978], pp. 360-69 and passim).

5. James Barr, in his *Fundamentalism* (see note 4, above), provides much evidence to show that the principal difference between "liberals" and "conservatives" too often is not so much *what* they believe, but rather *when* they believe. Frequently in the history of biblical interpretation conservatives come to accept "liberal" conclusions, but ten or a hundred years—or even centuries—after they are originally proposed. Conservative exegetes and theologians, virtually by definition, are not very creative in theology: they like to look to the rich heritage of the past and serve more as anchors than sails. Nevertheless they play an essential role in the life of the church, despite Barr's (often well-taken) criticisms (Eph. 4:14). Although I admire the creativity of many liberal scholars, I must also recognize that many of the "trial balloons" (critical hypotheses) launched with so much acclaim from Germany are quickly shot down there, never even crossing the English Channel to receive their appropriate correction. Meanwhile pastors in the church must seek to nourish their flock on solid food (Heb. 13:9), not trial balloons. The importance of Barr's book for conservatives is unintentionally suggested by the fact that Carl F. H. Henry gave it an unprecedented critical review in three installments, "Those Incomprehensible British Fundamentalists," *Christianity Today* (June 2, June 23, July 21, 1978). Despite Henry's many valid objections and corrections, the reading of his refutation should not substitute for reading Barr's work itself, which has much to teach conservatives. As William F. Wells noted in a parallel (and more balanced) review of Barr's book, "the work deserves a careful reading. Given the extent of his research, the quality of his sources, and the cogency of at least some of his arguments, his critical appraisal of the conservative perspective should not be ignored" (*Christianity Today*, June 2, 1978, p. 30).

6. *Liberation*, p. 9.

7. Julio de Santa Ana, *El Desafío de los Pobres a la Iglesia* (San José: EDUCA, 1977), pp. 63-67; in English see Julio de Santa Ana, *Good News to the Poor: The Challenge of the Poor in the History of the Church* (Maryknoll, N.Y.: Orbis Books,

1979). Luis Fernando Rivera, "Sobre el socialismo de Santiago (Sant. 2:1–13)" in Equipo SELADOC, *Panorama de la teología latinoamericana*, vol. 1 (Salamanca: Sígueme, 1975), pp. 63–67.

8. Greek lexicons and other authorities give as the first or primary meaning of *thlĩpsis* "oppression," not "affliction." For further details see the next section in this chapter and note 10, below.

9. *Pace* John R.W. Stott, "salvation" here is physical healing and is *distinguished* from forgiveness of sins. Stott does well, however, to point out the link between the hermeneutics of pentecostalism and liberation theologies (healing and political liberation). Also Stott correctly insists that we distinguish between the benefits always guaranteed to believers in this life (justification, sanctification, etc.) and those benefits secured in principle through the cross and resurrection, but often not fully enjoyed by the believer before death or the second coming. Cf. Stott's *Christian Mission in the Modern World* (Downers Grove, Ill.: InterVarsity Press, 1976), pp. 82–101. In biblical theology terms such as "salvation" and "kingdom of God" represent complex, multifaceted realities. To slice out sections of the total biblical reality and pretend that our favorite slice is all there is does nothing to preserve orthodoxy, but rather kills orthopraxis. For more faithful representation of the total biblical concepts of salvation and kingdom, see George E. Ladd, *Jesus and the Kingdom* (New York: Harper & Row, 1964) and Herman Ridderbos, *The Coming of the Kingdom* (Philadelphia: Presbyterian and Reformed Publ. Co., 1962). Particularly Ridderbos, with his Calvinistic emphasis on the continuity between Old and New Testaments, anticipates many of the exegetical conclusions and theological emphases of the liberation theologies.

10. William F. Arndt and F. Wilbur Gingrich, *A Greek-English Lexicon of the New Testament and other Early Christian Literature* (Chicago: University of Chicago Press, 1979), p. 362. See also "Persecution, Tribulation, Affliction" in *Dictionary of New Testament Theology,* Colin Brown, ed. (Grand Rapids: Zondervan, 1976), vol. 2, p. 807; Schlier, "Thlĩbo, Thlĩpsis" in *Theological Dictionary of the New Testament*, Gerhard Kittel, ed. (Grand Rapids: Eerdmans, 1965), vol. 3, p. 139.

11. The verb *thlĩbo* is translated "oppressed" (French: *opprimés*) in the Jerusalem Bible in Heb. 11:37. Perhaps this exception is motivated by the direct link with poverty in the context and because of the references to the Old Testament saints.

12. Juan B. Stam, "El Apocalipsis y el imperialismo" in *Capitalismo, Violencia y Anti-vida,* Elsa Tamez and Saúl Trinidad, eds. (San José: DEI-EDUCA, 1978), vol. 1, pp. 359–94.

13. "The linking of tribulation and poverty suggests a close connection between the two. In an antagonistic environment it would be difficult for the Christian to make a living, and thus many were economically destitute. They may also have been the victims of mob violence and looting (cf. Heb. 10:34)"; Robert H. Mounce, *The Book of Revelation* (Grand Rapids: Eerdmans, 1977), p. 92.

14. Philip Edgcombe Hughes, *A Commentary on the Epistle to the Hebrews* (Grand Rapids: Eerdmans, 1976), p. 92.

15. Hughes, *Hebrews*, pp. 426–31.

16. *Biblical Essays* (London: Macmillan, 1892), pp. 247–48.

17. Kittel, *Dictionary,* vol. 3, p. 147.

18. Kittel, ibid., p. 149, and Brown, *Dictionary,* vol. 2, p. 807, give much additional data concerning Hebrew roots for oppression translated by *thlĩpsis* and *thlĩbo*.

19. Kittel, *Dictionary,* vol. 3, p. 143, citing John 16:33; Acts 14:22; 1 Thess. 3:2–3; cf. 2 Tim. 3:12.

20. Ibid., pp. 146–47, and Brown, *Dictionary,* vol. 2, p. 807, point out other pertinent Greek terms: *anánkē, stenochōra, stenochōréō, lúpē, diōgmós, diókō,* etc.

21. *Thlīpsis* ("oppression, affliction") occurs 6 times in Acts (7:10–11; 11:19; 14:22; 22:23). It does not occur in Luke, but the other synoptic gospels have it seven times (Matt. 13:21 // Mark 4:17; Matt. 24:9, 21, 29 // Mark 24:19, 24).

22. *The New Testament Documents: Are They Reliable?* (London: Inter-Varsity, 5th ed., 1960), passim.

23. F. F. Bruce, *Commentary on the Book of Acts* (Grand Rapids: Eerdmans, 1954), pp. 2–24. Ernst Haenchen, *The Acts of the Apostles* (Philadelphia: Westminster, 1971), pp. 102–3.

24. *Liberation,* p. 95.

25. Ibid, p. 111–12.

26. For more details regarding the interpretation of this text, see the exegesis in chap. 7, below.

27. *Kingdom,* p. 188.

28. Ibid., p. 191. Note how far Ridderbos's integral interpretation is from Stott's dichotomistic conclusion that the salvation in the New Testament "is not socio-political liberation" (*Christian Mission,* p. 88).

29. "Poor" in Brown, *Dictionary,* vol. 2, pp. 820–29.

30. Segundo, *Liberation,* p. 11.

31. See Eph. 6 and the theme of the "powers" in Marcus Barth, *Ephesians,* Anchor Bible (Garden City, N.Y.: Doubleday, 1974), vol. 2, pp. 800–805. Also John R.W. Stott has an excellent summary and critique of modern studies on this theme in *God's New Society: The Message of Ephesians* (Downers Grove, Ill.: InterVarsity, 1980), pp. 267–75.

32. Although they are not presented so schematically, we find many of the same elements also in Luke's Gospel. For example, in Luke 9:1–19 Jesus sends out the twelve to heal and proclaim the kingdom (9:1–2), to identify fully with the poor in their lifestyle (9:3–5); then the news of their proclamation and miracles provokes Herod (9:7–9).

33. A definite linguistic link between oppression and persecution exists in biblical theology. See the study of *thlīpsis* and *thlíbo* in the preceding section and note 18, above.

34. On this theme, see K. F. Nickle, *The Collection: A Study in Paul's Strategy* (London: SCM Press, 1966).

35. Brown, *Dictionary,* vol. 2, pp. 295–304; Matt. 5:5, 10; Rom. 4:13; 1 Pet. 1:14.

36. Cf. also Col. 1:12–14.

37. *Pace* Stott, *Christian Mission,* pp. 82–101.

38. *Liberation,* p. 113.

39. See Eduardo Galeano, *Las venas abiertas de América Latina* (México City: Siglo Veintiuno, 2nd ed., 1973); in English, *The Open Veins of Latin America* (New York: Monthly Review, 1973).

40. See Elsa Tamez, *Bible of the Oppressed* (Maryknoll, N.Y.: Orbis, 1982). Penny Lernoux, *Cry of the People: United States Involvement in the Rise of Fascism, Torture and Murder and the Persecution of the Catholic Church in Latin America* (New York: Doubleday, 1980).

CHAPTER 4

1. Among evangelicals in the last it century was the great virtue of Franz Delitzsch to recognize that although much higher criticism was nurtured in the "swaddling clothes" of rationalism, certain nineteenth-century scholars in fact "raised it to the eminence of a science" (*Isaiah*, vol. 1, p. 38). This of course does not mean we should treat its working hypotheses as infallible or regard it as a "sacred cow." For so many conservatives even to the present, however, "higher criticism" is viewed as fundamentally diabolical—on a spiritual level with voodoo and witchcraft. And since no one wants to become too familiar with the spirits "who chirp and mutter" (Isa. 8:19), the data continually scrutinized in higher critical studies are surveyed superficially by conservative Evangelicals—kept at arm's length, so to speak. Consequently conservatives in many basic areas have never shown an understanding of the *problems* uncovered in higher critical studies, much less proposed satisfactory alternative answers. Not able to understand why their "solutions" are not taken seriously in scientific circles, they content themselves with impugning the spiritual condition, motives, and presuppositions of the critics. They need to return to the point of "derailment," understand *why* Delitzsch shifted, and learn to follow his very sane counsel regarding scientific investigation of the Old Testament. See now the extreme dissatisfaction with the present state of affairs exemplified by *both* sides in the so-called Maier-Stuhlmacher debate: Gerhard Maier, *The End of the Historical-Critical Method* (St. Louis: Concordia, 1977); Peter Stuhlmacher, *Historical Criticism and Theological Interpretation of Scripture* (Philadelphia: Fortress, 1977). See too the discussion by D. A. Carson, "Hermeneutics: A Brief Assessment of Some Trends," *Themelios* 2 (Jan. 1980) 18–19.

2. See José Míguez Bonino, *Christians and Marxists: The Mutual Challenge to Revolution* (Grand Rapids: Eerdmans, 1974), pp. 92 f., 129, 131 f.; *Doing Theology in a Revolutionary Situation* (Philadelphia: Fortress, 1975), pp. 106–31. Robert McAfee Brown, *Theology in a New Key* (Philadelphia: Westminster, 1978), pp. 67–70. As Míguez Bonino points out, Calvin shows a keen biblical awareness of class struggle that is strikingly absent in our later First World theologies. Tragically, Míguez Bonino's sane and highly perceptive works are often ignored by conservative-evangelical critics of the liberation theologies. Those eager to criticize and refute what they have not yet understood find easier targets in more extreme representatives of the liberation theologies. Catholic and Protestant theologies in the U.S.A. can just as easily be caricatured by citing out of context the sensational new works that draw media attention.

3. See Giulio Girardi, *Amor cristiano y lucha de clases* (Salamanca: Sígueme, 1975). Míguez Bonino, *Doing Theology*, pp. 106–31.

4. The paradigmatic significance of the exodus was a fundamental presupposition of much old Puritan theology in the U.S.A. Revered Puritan forefathers even went to the extreme of justifying the killing of "wicked Indians" from supposed parallels in Joshua's slaughter of the Canaanites! Unfortunately Brevard S. Childs's important commentary, *The Book of Exodus* (Philadelphia: Westminster, 1974), does not interact with either Puritan or liberation theologies. Still, its exegetical and historical perspectives are a good starting place. Scores of articles, especially in Spanish, provide other perspectives, some extreme. Sometimes in Latin America the ten plagues are understood as veiled references to guerrilla sabotage, as in Pablo Richard and Esteban

Torres, *Cristianismo, lucha ideológica y racionalidad socialista* (Salamanca: Sígueme, 1975), pp. 67–82. A saner, more common Latin American view is seen in Mortimer Arias, *Salvación es liberación* (Buenos Aires: Aurora, 1973), pp. 30–40, on "Redescubrimiento del Exodo." An early article of great influence is Leopoldo J. Nilus, "El Exodo como el Génesis de la Revolución," pp. 49–60, in Rubem Alves et al., *De la iglesia y la sociedad* (Montevideo: Tierra Nueva, 1971). From the perspective of biblical theology, John Howard Yoder makes some significant comments in "Probing the Meaning of Liberation," *Sojourners* (Sept. 1976), pp. 27–29. Norman K. Gottwald's *The Tribes of Yahweh* opens up countless new possibilities (Maryknoll, N.Y.: Orbis, 1979), pp. 191–219. For the paradigmatic function of the exodus in the New Testament numerous technical specialized articles have appeared in the journals. For starters consult the texts cited in R. E. Nixon, *The Exodus in the New Testament* (London: Tyndale, 1962). The significance of the exodus is *universalized*, not *spiritualized*, in the New Testament—a process already amply attested to in the Old. Francis Foulkes has a good summary of the paradigmatic development of the exodus in the prophets in *The Acts of God: A Study of the Basis of Typology in the Old Testament* (London: Tyndale, 1955), pp. 21–22. Key texts cited here: Hos. 2:14 f.; 7:16; 8:13 f.; 9:3, 6; 11:1, 5, 11; 12:9; Jer. 23:7 f.; 16:14 f.; Ezek. 20:34–36; Isa. 11:15; 24; 30:3; 51:10 f.; 52:3 f.; 41:18 f.; 43:17–20; 38:21; 49:10; 52:12. He omits the prophetic text on the theme most often cited in liberation theologies—Amos 9:7, which shows the exodus paradigm functioning in *gentile* history even in Old Testament times. Especially for critiques of certain extremes, see also S. Sabugal, in the next note (5) and Andrew J. Kirk, *Liberation Theology: An Evangelical View from the Third World* (Atlanta: John Knox, 1980), pp. 95–111, 147–52. Also of great value is the more recent work of E. A. Martens, *Plot and Purpose in the Old Testament* (Leicester: Inter-Varsity, 1981).

5. Mortimer Arias's work, cited in note 4, above, is a good introduction. A detailed work rich in biblical data and insight is S. Sabugal, *¿Liberación y secularización?* (Barcelona: Herder, 1978), pp. 15–40, 137–310. Although overly critical of the liberation theologies and seeking always to stress what he considers the "religious" dimension (a category not biblically defined and thus distorting his methodology), Sabugal is forced to conclude that salvation in the Bible is "an integral liberation of *all* the people, of the total person" (p. 40). See Sabugal's treatment of the exodus paradigm (pp. 41–122). In English, see the detailed survey in Colin Brown, ed., *Dictionary of New Testament Theology* (Grand Rapids: Zondervan, 1978), vol. 3, pp. 177–223 with bibliography. The correct interpretation of the biblical texts obviously remains a subject of great debate. Basically, it appears to revolve around the question of approaching the New Testament as fundamentally continuous with the Old or imposing as normative the material-spiritual dualism common in Greek philosophy. Particularly the heirs of Calvin (Reformed and covenant theologies) will have great difficulty avoiding the conclusion of the liberation theologies at this point.

6. Here the great work from the liberationist perspective is of course José P. Miranda's *Marx and the Bible* (Maryknoll, N.Y.: Orbis, 1974). That Miranda sometimes makes extreme statements does not permit us to ignore this extremely important contribution, filling in so many lacunas in traditional exegesis and biblical theology. I attempt to survey the biblical and theological data in my study, "El Reino y los pobres: perspectivas del Salmo 72," soon to be published in a work on the kingdom of God by the Seminario Bíblico Latinoamericano. On the theme of justice, comparison of traditional reformed theologies in the U.S.A. (Hodge, Buswell, et al.) with the Bible itself—or even the Dutch dogmaticians (Bavinck, Ridderbos)—is most

revealing regarding ideological control of exegetical conclusions. Democratization in the ownership and control of the means of production does not, of course, imply necessarily either centralized state ownership or the abolition of personal and family property. Many creative alternatives are developing in mixed economies. See Jacques Ellul, *Changer de révolution: L'inéluctable prolétariat* (Paris: Seuil, 1982).

7. Many years ago, teaching Jeremiah, I became aware of the fact that land is another of those fundamental biblical themes virtually untouched in First World theologies. It is the dominant theme in some 40 chapters in the Bible! Two excellent studies complement one another well: Javier Pikaza, *La Biblia y la teología de la historia: Tierra y promesa de Dios* (Madrid: Fax, 1972). Pikaza is unsurpassed for exegetical detail on land in both Testaments but weak theologically.Walter Brueggemann's *The Land* (Philadelphia: Fortress, 1977) is much better theologically, but misses much of Pikaza's exegetical underpinning. See also Antonio González Lamadrid, *La fuerza de la tierra* (Salamanca: Sígueme, 1981). As in the case of oppression, the relationship between the Old and New Testaments regarding land needs more study. To the dispensationalists belongs the credit of at least recognizing long ago that land is an important category in biblical theology. Unfortunately, this insight remained encased in eschatological speculation about Israel's promised return to the land. See Lewis Sperry Chafer, *Systematic Theology* (Dallas Seminary Press, 1948), vol. 4, pp. 318–20, 399, 427. Generally dispensationalist literal exegesis of the Old Testament anticipates many of the biblical emphases in the liberation theologies. Chafer (vol. 4, p. 322) even recognizes liberation from oppression as a basic feature of the Abrahamic covenant! Unfortunately, such insights are "domesticated" and rendered speculative and irrelevant by encasement in the rigid scheme of compartmentalized, discontinuous "dispensations." Thereby what was and will be (millennium) true for the nation Israel is rendered irrelevant for the church and society in the church age. This kind of platonistic spiritualizing, having been exorcised from Old Testament exegesis, enters with a vengeance into a New Testament house swept clean, with deplorable results; former terrorist Menachem Begin can oppress and terrorize homeless Palestinians at will because the prophecies are unconditionally Israel's. Covenant theologies in the Reformed tradition pursue the dynamic of continuity and development of biblical theology but often remain domesticated under the domination of Augustinian millennial spiritualizing. Biblical theology in a liberation context seeks to liberate exegesis from both types of oppression. Recently, however, conservative exegete Marten H. Woodstra admitted that "properly understood" the theology of land in Joshua "could be used to support a wholesome Liberation Theology, i.e., one in which the vertical dimension is not lacking." *The Book of Joshua* (Grand Rapids: Eerdmans, 1981), p. 36.

8. My Th.D. dissertation surveys the biblical vocabulary and usage much more thoroughly than the standard theological word books and other reference works: "The Theology of Divine Anger in the Psalms of Lament" (St Louis: Concordia Seminary, 1972), esp. pp. 51–313 (semantics). The wrath of God correlates primarily to injustice, oppression, and idolatry (the religion of the oppressor). The literature on prophetic denunciation is immense. Sabugal gives a good survey on denunciations as instruments of liberation (*¿Liberación?*, pp. 123–36).

9. The fundamental study here is Jon Sobrino, *Christology at the Crossroads: A Latin American Approach* (London: SCM; Maryknoll, N.Y.: Orbis, 1978). Sobrino's deviations from historical Evangelical understanding of the deity and death of Christ do not invalidate his many important contributions in areas where traditional theol-

ogies have suffered serious lacunae and distortions. Also significant (and including a wide variety of theological positions from diverse authors) is José Míguez Bonino et al., *Jesús: ni vencido ni monarca celestial* (Buenos Aires: Aurora/Tierra Nueva, 1977); English translation: *Faces of Jesus: Latin American Christologies* (Maryknoll, N.Y.: Orbis Books, forthcoming). More evangelical in orientation is Saul Trinidad, *Hacia una cristología* (San José: INDEF/Seminario Bíblico Latinoamericano, 1975). On ecclesiology, see especially the literature on *comunidades de base:* Sergio Torres and John Eagleson, eds., *The Challenge of Basic Christian Communities* (Maryknoll, N.Y.: Orbis, 1981).

10. On the replacement of the static Greek philosophical category of "ethics" with the dynamic biblical categories of "way" and "praxis," see Faustino Huamán Díaz, *"Derekh: Proyecto histórico de liberación-salvación* (San José: Seminario Bíblico Latinoamericano, 1983). For the liberation dimension in missiology, see Orlando E. Costas, *The Integrity of Mission* (New York: Harper & Row, 1979), esp. pp. 61–83.

11. Jürgen Moltmann's *Theology of Hope* (New York: Harper & Row, 1967) has influenced much biblical interpretation on this theme in Latin America. José P. Miranda's *Being and the Messiah* (Maryknoll, N.Y.: Orbis, 1977) stresses realized eschatology to the point of negating the second coming, but this is not typical. Juan Stam's article on the Book of Revelation is a good example of a more Evangelical orientation, stressing the neglected economico-political dimension and the this-world focus of the book: "El Apocalipsis y el imperialismo" in *Capitalismo: Violencia y anti-vida*, Elsa Támez and Saul Trinidad, eds. (San José: DEI, 1978), vol. 1, pp. 359–94. Cf. Míguez Bonino, *Doing Theology*, pp. 132–53.

12. J. Andrew Kirk, *Liberation Theology: An Evangelical View from the Third World* (Atlanta: John Knox Press, 1979), pp. 204, 207.

13. *East and West* (San Francisco: Harper & Row, 1980), pp. 39–71.

14. *Biblical Theology in Crisis* (Philadelphia: Westminster, 1970).

15. *God, Revelation and Authority* (Waco: Word, 1979).

CHAPTER 5

1. See E. J. Young, *Who Wrote Isaiah?* (Grand Rapids: Eerdmans, 1958); Gleason L. Archer, *A Survey of Old Testament Introduction* (Chicago: Moody Press, 2nd ed., 1974), pp. 326–51. Cracks continue to surface in the wall of defense of the traditional position. Franz Delitzsch, the great defender of the book's unity in the last century, eventually "leaped over the wall" and in the fourth edition of his classic commentary accepted the basic validity of the critical position: *Biblical Commentary on the Prophecies of Isaiah* (Edinburgh: Clark, 1980), vol. 1, pp. 36–41. J. Barton Payne recognized the problem of having a prophet not only address himself *to* an exilic community of a later century, but to do so *from* the apparent historical context of a later century and Babylonian locale. Such a feat, he admitted, would be contrary to the "analogy of prophecy": the prophets commonly speak *from* their historical context *to* their contemporaries (references to the near or distant future normally are included to bolster their message to their contemporaries—not as a kind of "science fiction"-type escape to another century). Hence Payne argued for an eighth-century Assyrian-dominated background of Isaiah 40–55. His arguments, however, only remind us how cruelly dogmatic theological suppositions can torture exegesis: "Eighth Century Israelitish Background of Isaiah 40–66," *Westminster Theological Journal* 29–30 (1967–68). R. K. Harrison argues for the essential unity of Isaiah (p. 784), but does not

believe such a conclusion can be established dogmatically and *a priori* by the New Testament references to the book (p. 793), and even regards the references naming the sixth-century Persian ruler Cyrus (Isa. 44:28; 45:1) as glosses (p. 794)!: *Introduction to the Old Testament* (Grand Rapids: Eerdmans, 1969). Dutch scholar N. H. Ridderbos committed the *faux pas* of following Delitzsch "over the wall" and admitting the essential validity of the critical position: *The New Bible Dictionary,* J. D. Douglas, ed. (London: Inter-Varsity Fellowship, 1962), p. 573. This lapse was rectified, however, for Inter-Varsity by Derek Kidner in the revised edition of the *New Bible Commentary,* D. Guthrie and J. A. Motyer, eds. (Downers Grove, Ill.: InterVarsity, 2nd ed., 1970), pp. 589–91. Kidner, however, sided with Ridderbos and Harrison in affirming that the question cannot be established *a priori* from the New Testament references and a belief in inerrancy. Kidner's major objection to the critical position, surprisingly enough, seems to be that it makes the interpretation of Isaiah too complicated (p. 590). One would think, however, that the exceeding complexity of that task had been abundantly established by most exegetical commentaries (Calvin, 4 volumes; E. J. Young, 3 volumes). F. F. Bruce and a growing number of conservative-evangelical scholars, especially in England and Holland, accept the basic validity of the critical analysis. They insist only that the critical conclusions be recognized for what they are: *working hypotheses,* not a new set of dogmas, and that the inspiration, utter truthfulness (many would accept the term "inerrancy"), and authority of the Scriptures as the word of God not be jeopardized by the acceptance of historico-critical analysis: "A Man of Unchanging Faith: An Interview with F. F. Bruce," *Christianity Today* (Oct. 10, 1980), pp. 16–18. The recent critical introduction of Brevard S. Childs makes startling concessions to conservative theological concerns with his emphasis on the final canonical form of the completed book: *Introduction to the Old Testament as Scripture* (Philadelphia: Fortress, 1979), pp. 311–38, esp. p. 325. Details of my own position are found in my article "Isaías," *Diccionario Ilustrado de la Biblia,* Wilton M. Nelson, ed. (Miami: Ed. Caribe, 1974), pp. 306–9.

2. *Isaiah 40–66* (Philadelphia: Westminster, 1969), p. 92; see also J. Albert Soggin, *Introduction to the Old Testament* (Philadelphia: Westminster, 1976), pp. 313–14; George Fohrer, *Introduction to the Old Testament* (Nashville: Abingdon, 1968), p. 387; Otto Kaiser, *Introduction to the Old Testament* (Minneapolis: Augsburg, 1975), pp. 266–67.

3. Some 46 words or expressions occur *only* in this song and not in the rest of Second Isaiah, according to Christopher R. North: *Suffering Servant in Deutero-Isaiah* (London: Oxford University Press, 2nd ed., 1956), p. 168. See Gerhard von Rad, *Old Testament Theology* (Edinburgh: Oliver and Boyd, 1972), vol. 2, pp. 250–62, 273–77, for the theology of suffering in the fourth song.

4. See Westermann, *Isaiah 40–66,* p. 257. Von Rad prefers to consider the Fourth Song as a "prophetic liturgy" that includes an elegy (*Old Testament Theology,* p. 255–56). In this he follows Sigmund Mowinckel ("a belated funeral dirge": *He That Cometh* [New York: Abingdon, 1954], p. 200).

5. Von Rad attributes all the Servant Songs to Second Isaiah (*Theology,* vol. 2, p. 251), as does James Muilenburg ("Isaiah: Chapters 40–66," *The Interpreter's Bible* [Nashville: Abingdon, 1956], vol. 5, pp. 465, 615). John L. McKenzie holds that all are from Third Isaiah (*Second Isaiah,* Anchor Bible [New York: Doubleday, 1968], p. xli).

6. Walter J. Hollenweger, *The Pentecostals* (Minneapolis: Augsburg, 1972), p. 515; see also pp. 359, 517, 521.

7. John R. W. Stott, *Christian Mission in the Modern World* (Downers Grove, Ill.: InterVarsity, 1975), pp. 84–88.

8. *Nueva Biblia Española* (Madrid: Ed. Cristiandad, 1975). The Vulgate reads *quasi leprosum*.

9. See Mowinckel, *He That Cometh*, p. 201.

10. This is the only definition in BDB (p. 318) and the first definition in Hol. (p. 105). Koehler translates "weakness, sickness," but sickness is a proper translation for all the 23 times the word occurs in the Old Testament: Deut. 7:15; 28:59, 61; 1 Kings 17:17; 2 Kings 1:2; 8:8, 9; 13:14; Isa. 1:5; 38:9; 53:3, 4; Jer. 6:7; 10:9; Hos. 5:13; Eccles. 5:16; 6:2; 2 Chron. 16:12 (twice); 21:15, 18-20; (Prov. 31:8 cj) (KB^2, p. 301).

11. Robert Horton Gundry, *The Use of the Old Testament in St. Matthew's Gospel* (Leiden: Brill, 1975), p. 111.

12. In order to broaden the meaning of healing, the NEB translates *shalom* in the parallel verse as "health": "The chastisement he bore is health *(shalom)* for us and by his scourging we are healed *(raph'a)."*

13. The best books I know on the theme are Francis MacNutt, *Healing* (Notre Dame: Ave Maria Press, 1974); *The Power to Heal* (Notre Dame: Ave Maria Press, 1977). He encourages expectant faith but avoids unbiblical fanaticism.

14. *The Book of Isaiah* (Grand Rapids: Eerdmans, 1975), vol. 3, p. 344.

15. See Wolfhart Pannenberg, *Jesus—God and Man* (London: SCM Press, 1968), p.278.

16. See Thomas Dixon Hanks, "The Theology of Divine Anger in the Psalms of Lament" (St. Louis: Concordia Seminary, 1972), pp. 4-5.

17. See Pannenberg, *Jesus,* pp. 278-79; Hanks, "Divine Anger," pp. 6-10.

18. See Hanks, "Divine Anger," pp. 10-11; Pannenberg, *Jesus,* p. 279.

19. See Hanks, "Divine Anger," pp. 11-13.

20. *Church Dogmatics*, IV:1 (New York: Scribner's, 1965), pp. 211-83.

21. *The Mediator* (London: Lutterworth, 1934), pp. 455-89.

22. C. G. Berkouwer, *The Work of Christ* (Grand Rapids: Eerdmans, 1956), pp. 135-80; G. Bloesch, *Essentials of Evangelical Theology* (New York: Harper & Row, 1978), vol. 1, pp. 148-80.

23. *Jesus,* pp. 278-80. See also Helmut Thieleke, *The Evangelical Faith* (Grand Rapids: Eerdmans, 1977), vol. 2, pp. 398-404.

24. *The Cross in the New Testament* (Grand Rapids: Eerdmans, 1965), passim.

25. *A Critical and Exegetical Commentary on the Epistle to the Romans* (Edinburgh: Clark, 1975), vol. 1, pp. 106-12, 214-18. See also C. K. Barrett, *Reading Through Romans* (Philadelphia: Fortress, 1977), p. 16; cf. Ernst Käsemann, *Commentary on Romans* (Grand Rapids: Eerdmans, 1980), pp. 91-101; John A. T. Robinson, *Wrestling with Romans* (Philadelphia: Westminster, 1979), pp. 44-46.

26. José Míguez Bonino, *Christians and Marxists* (Grand Rapids: Eerdmans, 1976), pp. 95-102.

27. The relationship between the "one" and the "many" is a frequent concern in this context, provoked by the population loss through invasion and exile: 49:19-21; 51:1-3, esp. 2; 53:10cd, 12ab; 54:1-13. *Many* had come from Abraham; but now they were *few*. Even those few are reduced to *one*—the faithful Servant in the fourth song. However descendants will come from him and later there will be a demographic explosion (Isa. 54).

28. *Biblical Commentary on the Prophecies of Isaiah* (Edinburgh: Clark, 4th ed., 1890), pp. 286-87. Cf. von Rad, *Theology,* vol. 2, p. 256.

29. *He That Cometh*, p. 202.

30. *Isaiah 40-66*, p. 263. Many words in Hebrew express penal substitution, punishment, etc. See W. S. Towner, "Retribution" in *Interpreter's Dictionary of the Bible:*

Supplementary Volume (Nashville: Abingdon, 1976), pp. 742–44; Isa. 53 in *Good News Bible: Today's English Version* (New York: American Bible Society, 1976). J. S. Whale observes: "the song makes twelve distinct and explicit statements that the Servant suffers the *penalty* of other men's sins" (*Victor and Victim: The Christian Doctrine of Redemption* [Cambridge: Cambridge University Press, 1960], p. 69).

31. G. Johannes Botterweck and Helmer Ringgren, eds., *Theological Dictionary of the Old Testament* (Grand Rapids: Eerdmans, 1974), vol. 1, pp. 443–44.

32. Ibid., p. 432; H. H. Rowley, *Worship in Ancient Israel* (Philadelphia: Fortress, 1967), pp. 127–31, 142–43.

33. See Botterweck-Ringgren, *Dictionary*, p. 433. Thus there is some exegetical basis for Anselm's emphasis on "satisfaction."

34. See Hanks, "Divine Anger," p. 162; Martin Noth, *Leviticus* (Philadelphia: Westminster, 1965), p. 24.

35. *Biblia Comentada* (Madrid: BAC, 1967), vol. 3, p. 320. We should note, however, that in the New Testament Paul (Rom. 3:25) prefers to speak of God's justice as "manifested" (a positive, outgoing expression), not as "satisfied" (Anselm). Similarly the verb "placate" may suggest more pagan than biblical concepts of divine anger.

36. See Morris, *The Cross*, pp. 323–25, 404–19.

37. Edward Gordon Selwyn, *The First Epistle of St. Peter* (London: MacMillan, 1955), p. 180.

38. See above, notes 15–25.

39. Mowinckel, *He That Cometh*, p. 199; Westermann, *Isaiah 40–66*, pp. 267–68.

40. Israel W. Slotki, *Isaiah,* Soncino Books of the Bible (London: Soncino, 1949), p. 264.

41. See E. Kautzsch and A.W. Cowley, eds., *Genenius' Hebrew Grammar* (Oxford: Clarendon Press, 1910), pp. 144 ff.

42. See Gerhard von Rad, "Faith Reckoned as Righteousness," *The Problem of the Hexateuch and Other Essays* (New York: McGraw-Hill, 1966), pp. 125–30.

43. Young, *Isaiah,* p. 357. See also Hans Küng, *Justification* (London: Nelson, 1964), pp. 208–21.

44. Cranfield, *Epistle to the Romans*, vol. 1, pp. 214–18.

45. *Christology at the Crossroads: A Latin American Approach* (Maryknoll, N.Y.: Orbis, 1978), p. 193.

46. KB², p. 604; Hol., p. 232.

47. Lev. 4:6, 12; 5:9; 6:20 (twice); 8:11, 30; 14:7, 16, 17, 51; 16:14 (twice), 15, 19.

48. See von Rad, *Theology*, vol. 2, p. 254.

49. "Isaiah," in the *Interpreter's Bible* p. 618.

50. *Theology*, vol. 2, p. 254.

51. Gerhard Kittel and Gerhard Friedrich, eds., *Theological Dictionary of the New Testament* (Grand Rapids: Eerdmans, 1968), vol. 6, pp. 977–84.

52. *Isaiah*, vol. 3, pp. 336–37. See also his *Studies in Isaiah* (Grand Rapids: Eerdmans, 1954), pp. 199–206.

53. See García Cordero, *Biblia Comentada*, pp. 322–23.

54. See H. H. Rowley, *The Servant of the Lord and Other Essays on the Old Testament* (Oxford: Blackwell, 2nd ed., 1965), p. 54; von Rad, *Theology*, vol. 2, p. 260.

55. *Servant*, pp. 51–60.

56. Well-informed conservatives such as Young recognize that an individualistic interpretation is not adequate: *Isaiah*, vol. 3, p. 109, note 1.

57. *Servant*, pp. 58-59.

58. *Isaiah 40-66*, p. 265.

59. *Christus Victor* (London: SPCK, 1953), passim. Cf. J. S. Whale, *Victor and Victim*, pp. 20-41; G. C. Berkouwer, *The Work of Christ*, pp. 327-42.

60. See Gundry, *Use of the Old Testament*, p. 146. Mowinckel points out that nowhere else in the Old or New Testament do these words occur in parallelism (*He That Cometh*, p. 201).

61. See Gundry, *Use of the Old Testament,* p. 146; McKenzie, *Second Isaiah*, p. 131; Young, *Isaiah*, vol. 3, pp. 352-53.

62. Mowinckel, *He That Cometh*, pp. 204 ff.

63. See Mitchell Dahood, *Psalms 1-50*, Anchor Bible (New York: Doubleday, 1966), pp. 221-33. I have translated: "he'll witness the dawn of liberation and be satisfied." "To see light" simply means to experience salvation or deliverance (Isa. 9:1[2]; 53:11 in the LXX and 1QIsᵃ, according to the article on *'ôr* in Botterweck-Ringgren, *Dictionary,* vol. 1, p. 161). See F. Asencio, *El Dios de la luz* (Rome: Gregorian University, 1958). pp. 133-50. Should the link between light and liberation common in Isaiah and John (8:12, 32, 36) be permitted to challenge traditional interpretations of 1 John (both liberal and conservative), the results would be startling. Liberal commentators stress that God is love (1 John 4:8, 16), forgetting that first he is light (1:5). Conservatives stress that God is light, but forget that light means liberation from oppression. John insists: "the darkness is passing and the true light [of liberation] is already shining" (1 John 2:8). See John Stott, *The Epistles of John* (Grand Rapids: Eerdmans, 1964), pp. 70-72; I. Howard Marshall, *The Epistles of John* (Grand Rapids: Eerdmans, 1978), p. 109; also the article "Phōs" (light) in Colin Brown, ed., *Dictionary of New Testament Theology* (Grand Rapids: Zondervan, 1976), vol. 2, pp. 490-96.

64. Jürgen Moltmann *El Dios Crucificado* (Salamanca: Sígueme, 1975), p. 461; in English, *The Crucified God* (New York: Harper and Row, 1974). See Dayton Roberts, *Running Out* (Glendale, Calif.: Gospel Light, 1975).

65. *Isaiah 40-66*, p. 269.

66. Ibid.,

67. *Isaiah*, vol. 3, p. 359.

68. "La actuación histórica del poder de Cristo," in *Jesús: ni vencido ni monarca celestial,* José Míguez Bonino, ed. (Buenos Aires: Aurora, 1977), pp. 196 ff. in English, *The Faces of God: Latin American Christologies* (Maryknoll, N.Y.: Orbis Books, forthcoming).

69. Ibid., p. 201.

70. For an outstanding contextualized (U.S.A.) interpretation of conversion and historical undertakings see Jim Wallis, *The Call to Conversion* (San Francisco: Harper and Row, 1981).

CHAPTER 6

1. *Jesus and the Old Testament* (London: Tyndale, 1971), p. 134.

2. *Luke: Historian and Theologian* (Grand Rapids: Zondervan, 1971), p. 184.

3. Ibid., p. 119; see also his commentary, *The Gospel of Luke* (Exeter: Paternoster, 1978), p. 182. Hugh Anderson concludes that Luke probably quoted freely and from

memory the LXX text of Isa. 61:1–2 and inserted Isa. 58:6c as a substitute for the reference to a day of vengeance (Isa. 61:2): "Luke believed that, on its rejection by the Jews, the gospel was sent to the Gentiles. We may therefore detect in the shape and form of the Isaianic citation of Luke 4:18–19 Luke's own hand and Luke's own theological viewpoint" ("Broadening Horizons: The Rejection at Nazareth Pericope of Luke 4:16–30 in Light of Recent Critical Trends," *Interpretation,* 18/3 [July 1964]: 269).

    4. Yet France says, "The occasion is the beginning of Jesus' public ministry and the quotation is, as it were, a manifesto, setting out his programme" (*Jesus and the Old Testament*, p. 134). For some of the more recent literature, see Marshall, *Luke: Historian*, pp. 180–81.

    5. *Luke: Historian*, p. 184.

    6. Claus Westermann, *Isaiah 40–60: A Commentary* (Philadelphia: Westminster, 1969), pp. 366–67. See also Edward J. Young, *The Book of Isaiah* (Grand Rapids: Eerdmans, 1972), vol. 3, p. 459. The grounds for seeing in Isa. 61:1–2 a reference to the Jubilee are fairly obvious: (1) The prophetic message is directed particularly to the poor, many of whom are also imprisoned (probably for debt). (2) The Hebrew word *deror* ("release, manumission [of slaves]," KB², p. 217) occurs only 7 times in the Old Testament (Lev. 25:10; Jer. 34:8, 15, 17 [twice]; Ezek. 46:17; Isa. 61:1), usually, if not always, as a reference to the Jubilee. The Jeremiah references may be disputed, but obviously refer to an event that exceeds the provisions of the sabbatical year. (3) When *deror* is coupled with the verb *qara'* (proclaim), the reference to the Jubilee is even clearer. (4) The reference in Isa. 61:2 to the proclamation of an acceptable *year* of Yahweh would appear to clinch the case. Only the Jubilee laws can account for all these factors. See Robert North, *Sociology of the Biblical Jubilee* (Rome: Pontificio Instituto Biblico, 1954), p. 228; Robert B. Sloan, Jr., *The Favorable Year of the Lord: A Study of Jubilary Theology in the Gospel of Luke* (Austin: Schola, 1977), pp. 4–18, 111–21.

    7. See Sloan, *Favorable Year,* pp. 40, 116.

    8. *Isaiah 40–66,* p. 340; cf. Sloan, *Favorable Year*, p. 116.

    9. *Isaiah 40–66,* p. 335.

    10. Cited by Westermann, ibid., p. 334.

    11. See Sloan, *Favorable Year*, p. 199, note 62.

    12. See A. van Selms, "Jubilee, Year of" in *The Interpreter's Dictionary of the Bible: Supplementary Volume* (New York: Abingdon, 1976), p. 497; R. K. Harrison, *Leviticus* (Downers Grover, Ill.: InterVarsity, 1980), pp. 228–29; G. W. Wenham, *The Book of Leviticus* (Grand Rapids: Eerdmans, 1979), p. 318.

    13. *Isaiah 40–66*, p. 337.

    14. The NEB destroys the beautiful progression of the Hebrew poetry, reversing the order of the last three lines to read: "to untie the knots of the yoke, to snap every yoke, and set free those who have been crushed." This gains in neat parallelism (yoke bars in successive lines) and gives us the resolution of the metaphor in a climactic last line. But surely the point of the Hebrew order is that the animal is first gently and carefully freed—and only then are the yoke bars violently smashed, to prevent a return to slavery (as happened in Jeremiah's time; Jer. 34).

    15. In the case of Jer. 34, when freeing of slaves was long overdue and a general emancipation proclaimed, inevitably it took on much of the essential character of the Jubilee Year, whatever the date or occasion. See John Bright, *Jeremiah,* Anchor Bible (Garden City, N.Y.: Doubleday, 1965), pp. 223–24; J. A. Thompson, *The Book of Jeremiah* (Grand Rapids: Eerdmans, 1980), pp. 608–13.

16. *Isaiah 40–66,* p. 337.

17. Ibid. On the relationship between the exodus paradigm and Jubilee, see also Sloan, *Favorable Year,* p. 9.

18. See Martin Noth, *Leviticus: A Commentary* (Philadelphia: Westminster, 1965), p. 191; but see also p. 189.

19. See Westermann, *Isaiah 40–66,* p. 337; cf. Matt. 25:31–46.

20. Young, *Isaiah,* vol. 3, p. 418. Note that here, as elsewhere in Scripture, the violence condemned is that of the oppressors, not that of the poor in their use of force to defend themselves.

21. Cited in Westermann, *Isaiah 40–66,* p. 336. Cf. KB², p. 276 *('atsãb),* p. 674 *('abat).*

22. The Hebrew *nagash* may bear the sense of "exact (a contribution)" or "press (a debtor for payment), dun" (KB², p. 594).

23. Volz, cited by James Muilenbergh, "Isaiah" in *The Interpreter's Bible* (New York: Abingdon, 1956), vol. 5, p. 652.

24. Marshall, *Luke: Historian,* p. 184.

25. Sloan, *Favorable Year,* pp. 118–21.

26. This feature of Isa. 58 well illustrates the oft-cited dictum of Latin American liberation theology: "The Exodus did not remain as a past experience, something that happened at a particular time in a particular place. It became the paradigm for the interpretation of all space and all time" (Rubem Alves, quoted in Hugo Assmann, *Theology for a Nomad Church* [Maryknoll, N.Y.: Orbis, 1975], p. 66).

27. See John Howard Yoder, *The Politics of Jesus* (Grand Rapids: Eerdmans, 1972), pp. 64–77; Sloan, *Favorable Year,* passim.

28. B. Z. Wacholder, "Sabbatical Year" in *The Interpreter's Dictionary of the Bible: Supplementary Volume* (New York: Abingdon, 1976), p. 762.

29. Marshall, *Luke: Historian,* pp. 119, 182. Jesus may well have quoted at length (and then preached) from both Isa. 58 and 61. Luke, or the Christian exegetical activity he incorporates, may give us only the key texts.

30. It is notable that a similar linking of Isa. 61:1–2 with another prophetic text—namely, Isa. 35:5–6—occurs in Luke 7:22. Again Luke appears to attribute the linking to Jesus himself.

31. "Jubilee," p. 498, italics added.

32. See North, *Biblical Jubilee,* passim; Sloan, *Favorable Year,* passim. Wenham recognizes that Lev. 25 condemns "the monopolistic tendencies of unbridled capitalism" (*Leviticus,* p. 323); see also his discerning comments on family and state. Cf. Harrison, *Leviticus,* p. 229.

33. Isa. 5:8; cf. Mic. 2:2; Amos 8:4.

34. As Calvin realized, the Jubilee laws are an exposition or explication of the eighth commandment (*Commentaries on the Last Four Books of Moses* [Grand Rapids: Eerdmans, 1950], vol. 3, pp. 162–71; see vol. 2, pp. 450–51, on the Sabbath).

35. Ronald J. Sider, *Rich Christians in a Hungry World* (Downers Grove, Ill.: InterVarsity, 1977), passim. In 2 Cor. 8:9, Paul makes it clear that Jesus' poverty is not a peripheral matter of "social ethics," but intrinsic to the gospel itself. See José Míguez Bonino, *Christians and Marxists* (Grand Rapids: Eerdmans, 1976).

36. Carl F. H. Henry asks, "Have evangelical Christians perhaps sacrificed to Marxists and religious humanists what stands at the heart of the Bible, namely a profound sense of social concern for a radically different society?" (*God, Revelation and Authority* [Waco: Word, 1979], vol. 4, p. 573). He admits that "Not only Latin

American Catholicism for four centuries, but Protestant missions also during the present century, have largely accommodated themselves to the social plight of the masses" (p. 575). Emilio Nuñez, professor at the dispensationalist Central American Theological Seminary, Guatemala, says: "We have to admit that traditional capitalism has not been able to solve our problems; that generally speaking, the rich are getting richer, and the poor, poorer in Latin American society. . . . We conservative evangelicals in Latin America have usually been concerned only about the individual, without taking into consideration his social context. We have been preaching about the spiritual element in man, without really paying attention to his physical and material needs. We have been preaching about heaven and hell, without declaring the totality of the counsel of God in relation to life this side of the grave. We have been denouncing the sinfulness of the individual, but not the evils of society as a whole. Our message has not been a threat to people in the wealthy class, in government, in the military. We conservative evangelicals in Latin America are known as 'good people,' because we do not interfere in political affairs, and do not make the people aware of their need of total liberation. Dictators have loved us and protected us for almost a century, in Central America, because of our non-involvement in politics. Of course, our non-involvement has been a political option, by which we have contributed to the preservation of the status quo in Latin American society" ("The Challenge of Liberation Theology," *Evangelical Missions Quarterly*, July 1981, pp. 41–42).

37. *Violence: Reflections from a Christian Perspective* (London: SCM Press, 1970).
38. *Amor cristiano y lucha de clases* (Salamanca: Sígueme, 1971).
39. *The Violence Inside* (London: SCM Press, 1978).
40. *Violence,* p. 159.
41. See Ellul, *Violence,* pp. 127–75.
42. See Gerhard von Rad, *Old Testament Theology* (Edinburgh: Oliver and Boyd, 1972), vol. 2, p. 315.
43. Three other significant works on violence: Hannah Arendt, *On Violence* (New York: Harcourt, Brace & World, 1969); Os Guiness, *Violence, A Study of Contemporary Attitudes* (Downers Grove, Ill.: InterVarsity, 1974); H. J. Steobe, "Violencia" in *Diccionario Teológico Manual del Antiguo Testamento,* Ernst Jenni and Claus Westermann, eds. (Madrid: Ed. Cristiandad, 1978). My basic contentions regarding *ḥamas* are now amply confirmed by the work of Jacques Pons (pp. 27–52) discussed briefly above (chap. 1, note 29).

CHAPTER 7

1. See, for example, the works of Karl Marx and Friedrich Engels in the collection *On Religion* (New York: Schocken, 1964), esp. pp. 101, 205–6, 316.
2. See José Míguez Bonino, *Christians and Marxists: The Mutual Challenge to Revolution* (Grand Rapids: Eerdmans, 1976).
3. Matt. 5:25, 26; 18:30; Luke 12:57–59. See Claus Westermann, *Isaiah 40–66: A Commentary* (Philadelphia: Westminster, 1969), p. 366. They are not "prisoners of war," as I. Howard Marshall claims (*The Gospel of Luke* [Exeter: Paternoster, 1978], p. 184).
4. See above, chaps. 1 and 2.
5. Luke 4:18; 7:21, 11; 14:13, 21; 18:35. Compare the Jubilee Year provision (Lev. 25:35; Isa. 58:7) for giving lodging to the homeless poor with Luke 14:13, 21.
6. But we should note that God himself ordered Moses to make such a long speech! See the context in Exod. 5:22–6:9.

7. John 1:1–3; Gen. 1:1 ff.

8. Cf. Luke 1:77; 3:3.

9. We find a powerful example of the way Jesus brings about awareness and strips away the Pharisees' hypocritical veneer in Matt. 23.

10. Lev. 25:10c; cf. vv. 35–55.

11. Lev. 25:10b; cf. vv. 13–18, 23–24.

12. Lev. 25:11, 12; cf. vv. 19–22. See also the laws for the Sabbath year in which the land was to rest once every seventh year, 25:1–7.

13. Marshall, *Gospel of Luke*, pp. 133, 184, and the literature he cites.

14. See also John Howard Yoder, *The Politics of Jesus* (Grand Rapids: Eerdmans, 1972), for a study of the Year of Jubilee in Jesus' teachings.

15. It is commonly accepted that Luke 4:19 and Isa. 61:2 refer to the Year of Jubilee. But what has not received much attention is that Isa. 58 does so also. Theologians have not been able to explain why Jesus interrupts his synagogue reading of Isa. 61:1–2 by inserting a short phrase from Isaiah 58 ("to let the oppressed go free"). Once we relate this to the provisions of the Jubilee legislation, the answer is obvious. Isa. 58 refers to the Year of Jubilee, as we can see for the following reasons: (1) Isa. 58 occurs in a setting in which the Sabbath receives much emphasis (56:1–2; 58:13–14). (2) Isa. 58 uses the Day of Atonement and a fast as its starting point and continues by announcing that Jubilee was the only fast called for in the Old Testament's legal calendar. (3) Isa. 58 repeats the basic provisions of the Year of Jubilee: freedom for debtors and the oppressed; sharing of bread with the poor; providing lodging, etc. (4) There are also many linguistic similarities between the chapters. For more details, see "Isaiah 58 and the Jubilee Year," in chap. 6, above.

16. John 2:13–22; Mark 11:15–17; Luke 19:45, 46; Matt. 21:12–13.

17. Mark 3:1–6; Matt. 23.

18. *Amor cristiano y lucha de clases* (Salamanca: Sígueme, 1975), p. 57.

19. For a Christian perspective on violence, see chap. 6 of José Míguez Bonino, *Doing Theology in a Revolutionary Situation* (Philadelphia: Fortress, 1975).

20. A propitiation is something that wards off or turns away anger. See Leon Morris, *The Apostolic Preaching of the Cross* (Grand Rapids: Eerdmans, 1956), pp. 125–85; C. E. B. Cranfield, *A Critical and Exegetical Commentary on the Epistle to the Romans* (Edinburgh: Clark, 1975), pp. 214–16.

21. E.g., Mark 8:31–34, where Peter tries to turn Jesus away from the road to Jerusalem and the cross.

22. George Matteson, 1890.

Index of Hebrew Words and Roots

147

Index of Biblical References

Only those references central to the author's argument are here included

Index of Authors and Topics

The Index was compiled by William E. Jerman